(45) (49)

P16

P18 Bésame mucho
20 Black Op.
24 Body + Soul
25
41
49
46
67
70
77

91 Misty
95 Favorite things
104
109
114
116   #24
139

THE JAZZ STANDARDS BOOK

ISBN 0-634-02665-8

HAL•LEONARD® CORPORATION

7777 W. BLUEMOUND RD. P.O. BOX 13819 MILWAUKEE, WI 53213

Visit Hal Leonard Online at
www.halleonard.com

JAZZ STANDARDS

THE BOOK

CONTENTS

STRUM AND PICK PATTERNS

This chart contains the suggested strum and pick patterns that are referred to by number at the beginning of each song in this book. The symbols ⊓ and ∨ in the strum patterns refer to down and up strokes, respectively. The letters in the pick patterns indicate which right-hand fingers plays which strings.

p = **thumb**
i = **index finger**
m = **middle finger**
a = **ring finger**

For example; Pick Pattern 2
is played: thumb - index - middle - ring

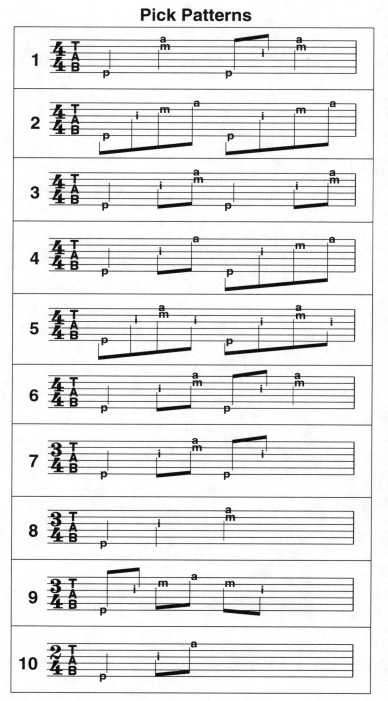

Strum Patterns

Pick Patterns

You can use the 3/4 Strum or Pick Patterns in songs written in compound meter (6/8, 9/8, 12/8, etc.).
For example, you can accompany a song in 6/8 by playing the 3/4 pattern twice in each measure.
The 4/4 Strum and Pick Patterns can be used for songs written in cut time (¢) by doubling the note time values in the patterns. Each pattern would therefore last two measures in cut time.

Ain't Misbehavin'

from AIN'T MISBEHAVIN'

Words by Andy Razaf
Music by Thomas "Fats" Waller and Harry Brooks

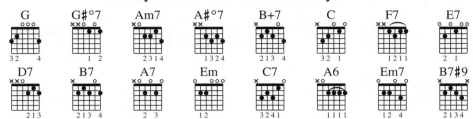

Strum Pattern: 4
Pick Pattern: 5

1. No one to talk with, all by my-self, no one to walk with, but
2., 3. *See Additional Lyrics*

I'm hap-py on ___ the shelf. Ain't mis-be-hav-in', I'm sav-in' my love for

you. ___ / you. ___

Bridge

Like Jack Hor-ner in the cor-ner, don't go no-where. What do I care? Your kiss-es

are worth wait-in' for, be-lieve me.

Coda

you. ___

Additional Lyrics

2. I know for certain the one I love,
   I'm thru with flirtin', it's just you I'm thinkin' of.
   Ain't misbehavin', I'm savin' my love for you.

3. I don't stay out late, don't care to go.
   I'm home about eight, just me and my radio.
   Ain't misbehavin', I'm savin' my love for you.

All of Me

Words and Music by Seymour Simons and Gerald Marks

Strum Pattern: 2, 5
Pick Pattern: 1, 4

Verse
Moderately

Alright, Okay, You Win

Words and Music by Sid Wyche and Mayme Watts

I'm in love with you. __ Well, al - right, __ o - kay, __

__ you win. __ Ba - by, what can I do? __ I'll __

__ do an - y - thing __ you say; __ sweet ba - by take me by the hand. __

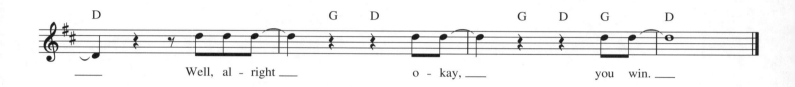

Well, al - right __ o - kay, __ you win. __

Always

Words and Music by Irving Berlin

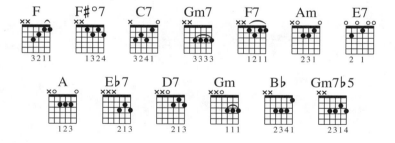

Strum Pattern: 7, 8
Pick Pattern: 8, 9

Verse
Moderately

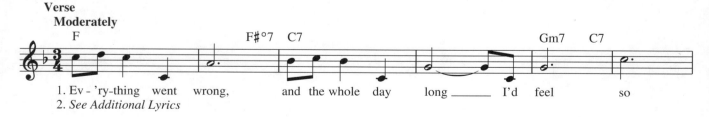

1. Ev - 'ry-thing went wrong, and the whole day long ___ I'd feel so
2. *See Additional Lyrics*

blue. ___ For the long - est while I'd for - get to smile. ___ Then

I met you. _____ Now that my blue days have

passed, _____ now that I've found you at last, _____

Chorus

I'll be lov-ing you, al - ways _____ with a love that's true,

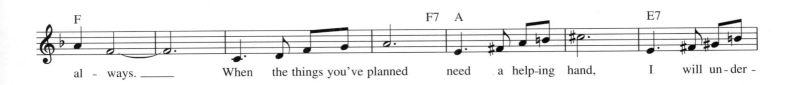

al - ways. _____ When the things you've planned need a help-ing hand, I will un-der-

stand, al - ways, al - ways. Days may not be fair, al - ways. _____

That's when I'll be there, al - ways, _____ not for just an hour, not for just a

day, not for just a year, but al - ways. _____ al - ways. _____

Additional Lyrics

2. Dreams will all come true, growing old with you,
   And time will fly,
   Caring each day more than the day before,
   Till spring rolls by.
   Then when the springtime has gone,
   Then will my love linger on.

9

Angel Eyes

Words by Earl Brent
Music by Matt Dennis

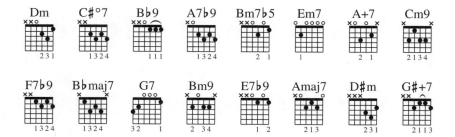

Strum Pattern: 6
Pick Pattern: 4

Intro
Moderately Slow
N.C.

Verse

Try to think _ that love's not a - round, _ still it's un - com - fort-'bly near. _

My old heart _ ain't gain - in' no ground _ be - cause my an - gel eyes ain't here. _

An - gel eyes _ that old dev - il sent, _ they glow un - bear - a - bly bright. _

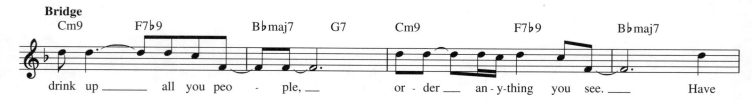

Need I say _ that my love's mis - spent, _ mis - spent with an - gel eyes to - night. _ So

Bridge

drink up _____ all you peo - ple, _ or - der _ an - y - thing you see. ___ Have

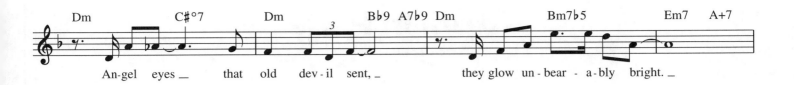

An-gel eyes __ that old dev-il sent, __ they glow un-bear-a-bly bright. __

Need I say __ that my love's mis-spent, __ mis-spent with an-gel eyes to-night. __ So

Bridge

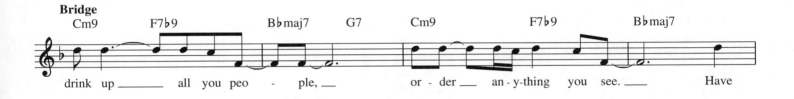

drink up _____ all you peo - ple, __ or-der __ an-y-thing you see. __ Have

fun, _____ you __ hap-py peo - ple, __ the drink and the laughs __ on me. __

Outro

Par-don me, __ but I got-ta run, __ the fact's un-com-mon-ly clear. __

Got-ta find __ who's now "Num-ber one" __ and why my an-gel eyes ain't here. __

'Scuse me while I dis-ap - pear. __

April in Paris

Words by E.Y. Harburg
Music by Vernon Duke

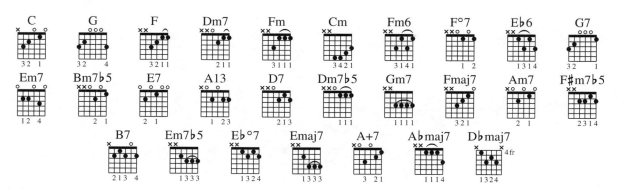

Strum Pattern: 3
Pick Pattern: 6

Verse
Moderately

A-pril's in the air, but here in Par - is A - pril wears a dif - f'rent gown.

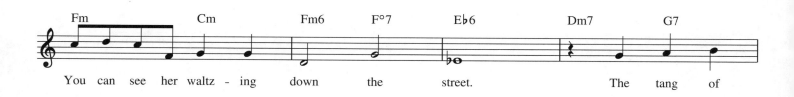

You can see her waltz - ing down the street. The tang of

wine is in the air, I'm drunk with all the hap - pi - ness that spring can give.

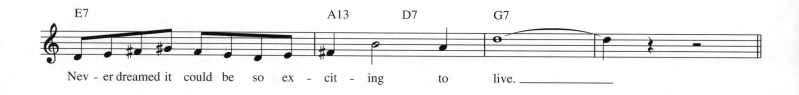

Nev - er dreamed it could be so ex - cit - ing to live. _____

Chorus

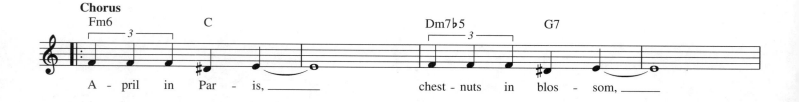

A - pril in Par - is, _____ chest - nuts in blos - som, _____

hol - i - day ta - bles un - der the trees. _____

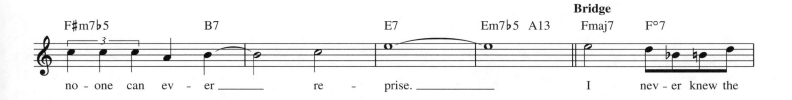
A - pril in Par - is, _____ this is a feel - ing _____

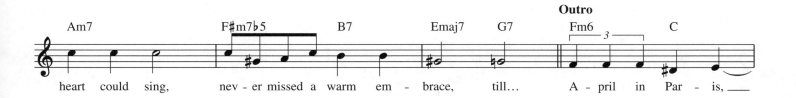
no - one can ev - er _____ re - prise. _____ I nev - er knew the

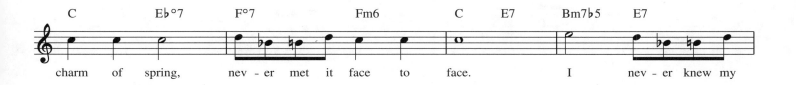
charm of spring, nev - er met it face to face. I nev - er knew my

heart could sing, nev - er missed a warm em - brace, till... A - pril in Par - is, ___

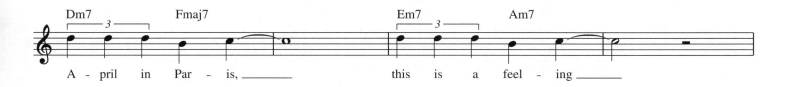
___ whom can I run to, _____ what have you done to _____

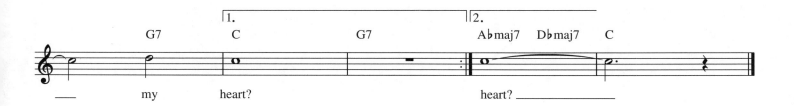
___ my heart? heart? _____

Autumn in New York

Words and Music by Vernon Duke

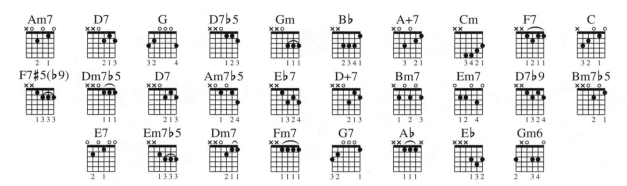

Strum Pattern: 3, 4
Pick Pattern: 3

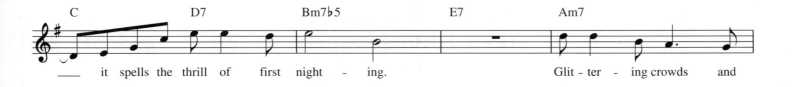

___ it spells the thrill of first night - ing. Glit - ter - ing crowds and

shim-mer - ing clouds in can - yons of steel, ___ they're mak - ing me feel ___

___ I'm home. ___ It's au - tumn in New York ___

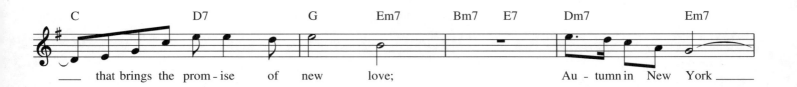

___ that brings the prom - ise of new love; Au - tumn in New York ___

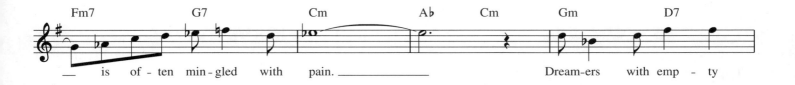

___ is of - ten min - gled with pain. ___ Dream-ers with emp - ty

hands may sigh for ex - o - tic lands; it's Au - tumn in New York, ___

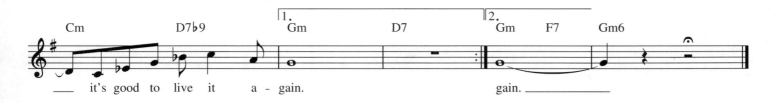

___ it's good to live it a - gain. gain. ___

Additional Lyrics

Chorus   Autumn in New York, the gleaming rooftops at sundown.
Autumn in New York, it lifts you up when you're rundown.
Jaded rove's and gay divorcees who lunch at the Ritz,
Will tell you that "it's divine!"
This autumn in New York transforms the slums into Mayfair;
Autumn in New York, you'll need no castles in Spain.
Lovers that bless the dark on benches in Central Park
Greet autumn in New York; it's good to live it again.

Autumn Leaves
(Les Feuilles Mortes)

English lyric by Johnny Mercer
French lyric by Jacques Prevert
Music by Joseph Kosma

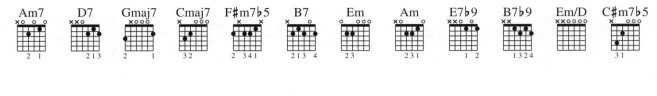

Strum Pattern: 3, 6
Pick Pattern: 1, 4

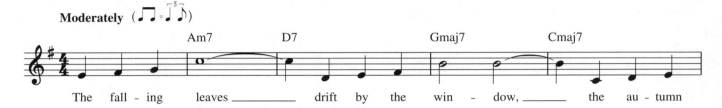

The fall - ing leaves _____ drift by the win - dow, _____ the au - tumn

leaves, _____ of red and gold. I see your lips, _____ the sum - mer

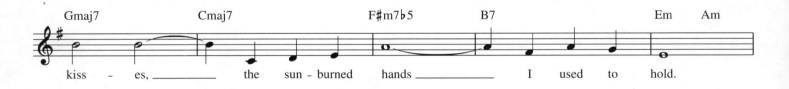

kiss - es, _____ the sun - burned hands _____ I used to hold.

Since you went a - way _____ the days grow long, _____ and soon I'll

hear _____ old win - ter's song. _____ But I miss you most of all my

dar - ling, _____ when au - tumn leaves start to fall. _____

Bewitched

from PAL JOEY
Words by Lorenz Hart
Music by Richard Rodgers

Strum Pattern: 2
Pick Pattern: 4

17

Bésame Mucho
(Kiss Me Much)

Music and Spanish Words by Consuelo Velazquez
English Words by Sunny Skylar

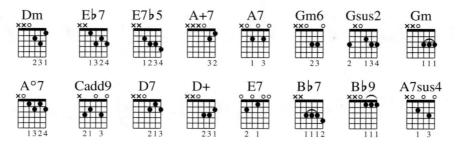

Strum Pattern: 1, 3
Pick Pattern: 2, 4

Intro
Moderately

Verse

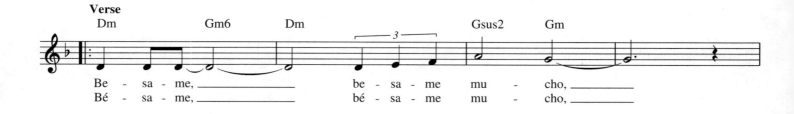

Be - sa - me, _____ be - sa - me mu - cho, _____
Bé - sa - me, _____ bé - sa - me mu - cho, _____

each time I cling to your kiss I hear mu - sic di - vine. _____
co - mo si fur - ra es - ta no - che la úl - ti - ma vez;

Be - sa - me mu - cho, _____
bé - sa - me mu - cho, _____

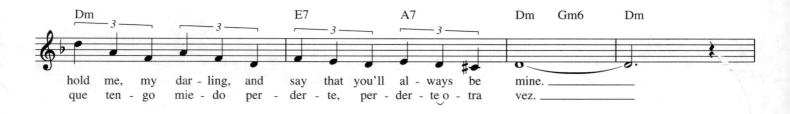

hold me, my dar - ling, and say that you'll al - ways be mine. _____
que ten - go mie - do per - der - te, per - der - te o - tra vez.

Gm / Dm / A7 / Gm6

This joy is some-thing new, my arms en-fold-ing you, nev-er knew this thrill be-
Quie-ro te-ner-te muy cer-ca, mi-rar-me en tus o-jos, ver-te jun-to a

Dm / Gm / Dm

fore. Who-ev-er thought I'd be hold-ing you close to me,
mí, pien-sa que tal vez ma-ña-na yo ya es-ta-ré

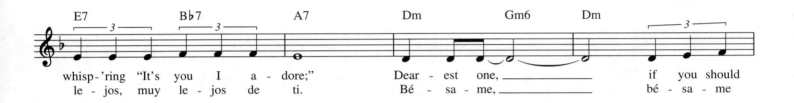

E7 / Bb7 / A7 / Dm / Gm6 / Dm

whisp-'ring "It's you I a-dore;" Dear-est one, _____ if you should
le-jos, muy le-jos de ti. Bé-sa-me, _____ bé-sa-me

Gsus2 / Gm / A°7 / Gm / A7

leave me, _____ each lit-tle dream would take wing and my life would be
mu-cho, _____ co-mo si fue-ra es-ta no-che la úl-ti-ma

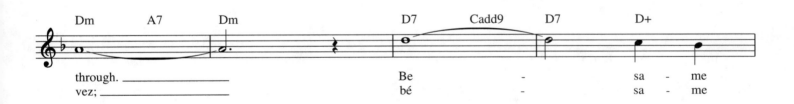

Dm / A7 / Dm / D7 / Cadd9 / D7 / D+

through. _____ Be - sa - me
vez; _____ bé - sa - me

Gsus2 / Gm / Dm / E7 / A7 / A+7

mu-cho, _____ love me for-ev-er and make all my dreams come
mu-cho, _____ que ten-go mie-do per-der-te, per-der-te des-

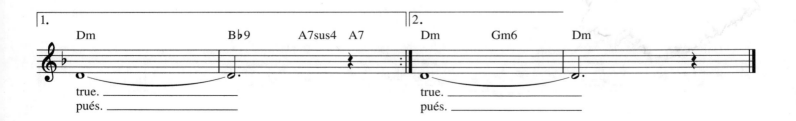

1.
Dm / Bb9 / A7sus4 A7 2. Dm / Gm6 / Dm

true. _____
pués. _____

true. _____
pués. _____

Black Orpheus

Words and Music Luiz Bonfa

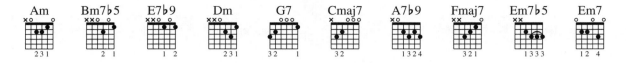

Strum Pattern: 3
Pick Pattern: 3

The Blue Room

from THE GIRL FRIEND

Words by Lorenz Hart
Music by Richard Rodgers

Strum Pattern: 6
Pick Pattern: 6

Verse
Slowly

1., 3. We'll have a blue room, a new room, for two room, where ev-'ry day's a hol-i-day be-cause you're mar-ried to me. Not like a ball-room, a small room, a hall room, where { I / you } can smoke { my / your }

Bridge

pipe a-way, with your wee head up on my knee. We will thrive on, keep a-live on just noth-ing but kiss-es, with Mis-ter and

Verse

Mis-ses on lit-tle blue chairs. { 2. You sew your / 4. I'll wear my } trou-seau and Rob-in-son Cru-soe is not so far from world-ly cares as our blue room far a-way up-stairs! stairs!

1.

2.

Blue Skies

from BETSY

Words and Music by Irving Berlin

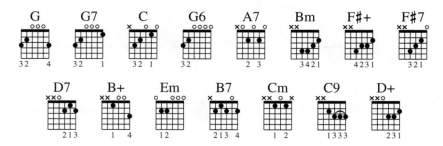

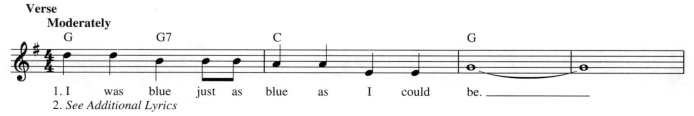

Strum Pattern: 3, 5
Pick Pattern: 3, 6

Verse
Moderately

1. I was blue just as blue as I could be. _____
2. *See Additional Lyrics*

Ev - 'ry day was a cloud - y day for me. _____

Then good luck came a - knock - ing at my door. _____

Skies were gray but they're not gray an - y - more. _____

Chorus

Blue skies _____ smil - ing at me. _____ Noth - ing but

blue skies _____ do I see. _____

Blue - birds _____ sing - ing a song; _____ noth - ing but

blue - birds _____ all day long. _____

Bridge

Nev - er saw the sun shin - ing so bright. Nev - er saw things go - ing so right.

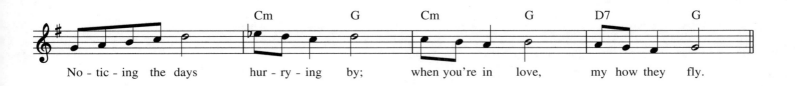

No - tic - ing the days hur - ry - ing by; when you're in love, my how they fly.

Outro

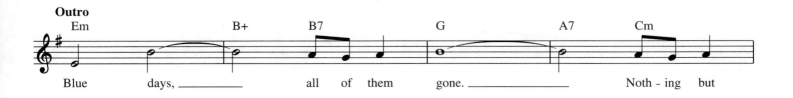

Blue days, _____ all of them gone. _____ Noth - ing but

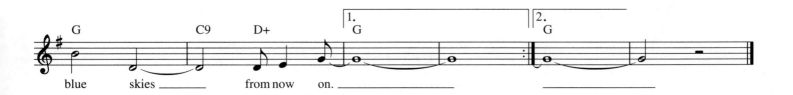

blue skies _____ from now on. _____ _____

Additional Lyrics

2. I should care if the wind blows east or west.
I should fret if the worst looks like the best.
I should mind if they say it can't be true.
I should smile if that's exactly what I do.

Body and Soul

Words by Edward Heyman, Robert Sour and Frank Eyton
Music by John Green

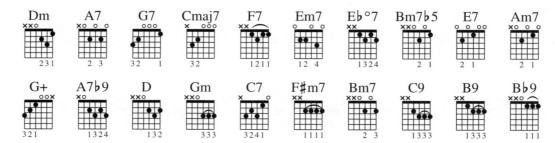

Strum Pattern: 4
Pick Pattern: 5

Verse
Slowly

1. My heart is sad and lone - ly, for you I sigh, for you, dear, on - ly.
2., 3. *See Additional Lyrics*

Why have-n't you seen it? I'm all for you, bod-y and soul!

soul! I can't be-lieve it, it's hard to con-ceive it that you'd turn a-way ro -

mance. Are you pre-tend-ing, it looks like the end-ing un-less I could have one more

chance to prove, dear.

soul!

Additional Lyrics

2. I spend my days in longing
   And wond'ring why it's me you're wronging,
   I tell you I mean it
   I'm all for you, body and soul!

3. My life a wreck you're making,
   You know I'm yours for just the taking;
   I'll gladly surrender
   Myself to you, body and soul!

But Beautiful

Words by Johnny Burke
Music by Jimmy Van Heusen

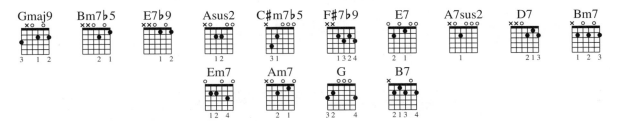

Strum Pattern: 2, 3
Pick Pattern: 3, 4

Verse

Slowly

1. Love is (3.) fun – ny or it's sad or it's qui – et or it's

mad; it's a good thing or it's bad, but beau – ti – ful! _____

Beau – ti – ful to take a chance and if you fall, you fall, and I'm

think – ing I would – n't mind at all. _____ 2., 4. Love is tear – ful or it's

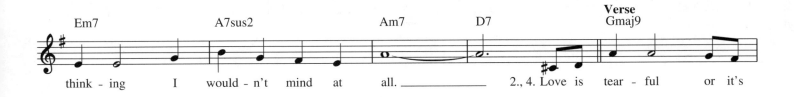

gay; it's a prob – lem or it's play; it's a heart – ache eith – er

way, but beau – ti – ful! _____ And I'm think – ing if

25

you were mine I'd nev-er let you go, and that would be but

beau-ti-ful I know. _____ 3. Love is know. _____

Bye Bye Blackbird

from PETE KELLY'S BLUES
Lyric by Mort Dixon
Music by Ray Henderson

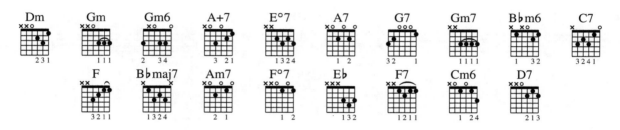

Strum Pattern: 3
Pick Pattern: 3

Verse
Moderately

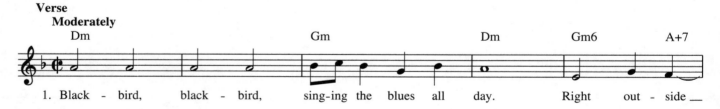

1. Black-bird, black-bird, sing-ing the blues all day. Right out-side _____

_____ of my door. _____ Black-bird, black-bird, got-ta be on my way,

Chorus

where there's sun-shine ga-lore. _____ Pack up all my care and woe, here I go.

Sing - ing low, bye bye black - bird, _____ where some-bod - y waits for me.

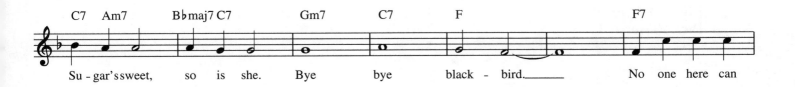

Su - gar's sweet, so is she. Bye bye black - bird._____ No one here can

love and un - der - stand me. Oh, what hard luck sto - ries they all hand

me; make my bed and light the light. I'll ar - rive late to - night,

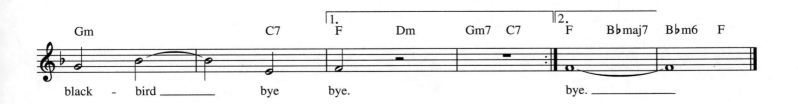

black - bird _____ bye bye. bye. _____

Additional Show Lyrics

Bluebird, bluebird, calling me far away.
I've been longing for you.
Bluebird, bluebird, this is my lucky day.
Now my dreams will come true.

Caravan

from SOPHISTICATED LADIES

Words and Music by Duke Ellington, Irving Mills and Juan Tizol

Strum Pattern: 3
Pick Pattern: 3

Additional Lyrics

2. Sleep upon my shoulder as we creep
Across the sands so I may keep
This memory of our caravan.

3. ...you, beside me here beneath the blue
My dream of love is coming true
Within our desert caravan.

Cherokee (Indian Love Song)

Words and Music by Ray Noble

Strum Pattern: 3
Pick Pattern: 3

29

Cheek to Cheek

from the RKO Radio Motion Picture TOP HAT

Words and Music by Irving Berlin

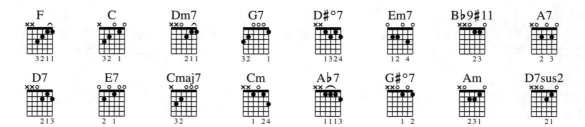

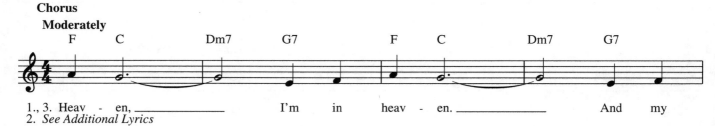

Strum Pattern: 4
Pick Pattern: 5

Chorus
Moderately

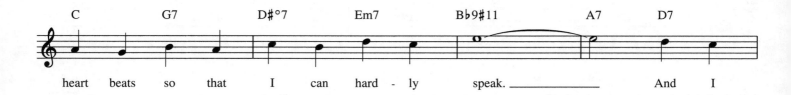

1., 3. Heav - en, _____ I'm in heav - en. _____ And my
2. *See Additional Lyrics*

heart beats so that I can hard - ly speak. _____ And I

seem to find the hap - pi - ness I seek. _____ when we're

To Coda ⊕

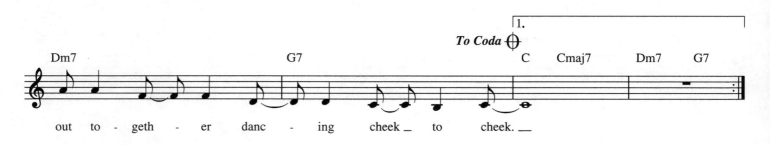

out to - geth - er danc - ing cheek __ to cheek. __

Verse

_____ 1. Oh, I love to climb a moun - tain, and to
2. *See Additional Lyrics*

reach the high-est peak. ___ But it does-n't thrill me half as much ___ as

1.   **2.**

danc - ing cheek to cheek. ___ 2. Oh, I ___

Bridge

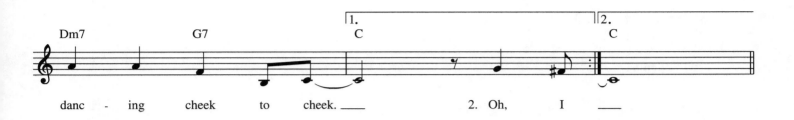

Dance with me. _____ I want my arm a - bout you. _____ The

D.C. al Coda

charm a - bout you _____ will car - ry me thru _____ to. . .

✲ *Coda*

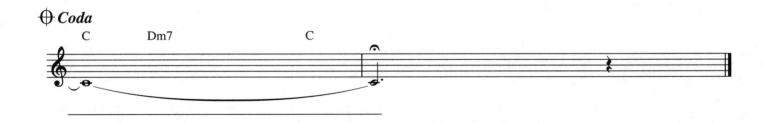

Additional Lyrics

Chorus   2. Heaven, I'm in heaven.
            And the cares that hung around me thru the week
            Seem to vanish like a gambler's lucky streak
            When we're out together dancing cheek to cheek.

        2. Oh, I love to go out fishing
            In a river or a creek.
            But I don't enjoy it half as much
            As dancing cheek to cheek.

Cherry Pink and Apple Blossom White

French Words by Jacques Larue
English Words by Mack David
Music by Louiguy

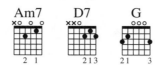

Strum Pattern: 1, 3
Pick Pattern: 2, 4

Verse

Rhumba

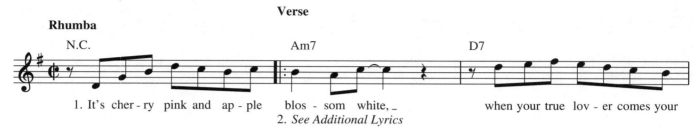

N.C. / Am7 / D7

1. It's cher - ry pink and ap - ple blos - som white, _ when your true lov - er comes your
2. *See Additional Lyrics*

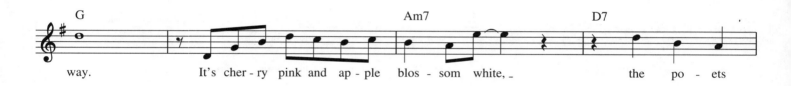

G / Am7 / D7

way. It's cher - ry pink and ap - ple blos - som white, _ the po - ets

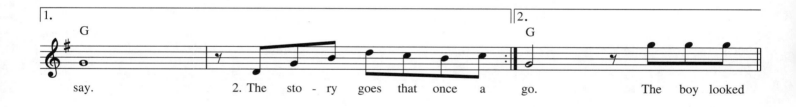

1. G / 2. G

say. 2. The sto - ry goes that once a go. The boy looked

Bridge

D7 / G / D7

in - to her eyes, it was a sight to en - thrall. The breez - es joined in their sighs, the blos - soms

G / D7 / G

start - ed to fall. And as they gent - ly ca - ressed, the lov - ers looked up to find, the branch - es

Outro

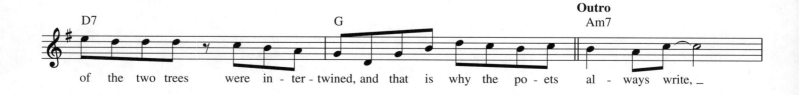

D7 / G / Am7

of the two trees were in - ter - twined, and that is why the po - ets al - ways write, _

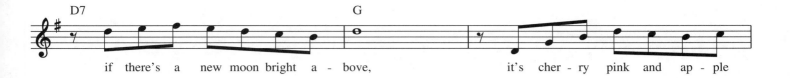

if there's a new moon bright a - bove,   it's cher - ry pink and ap - ple

blos - som white, __   when you're in love. _____

Additional Lyrics

2. The story goes that once a cherry tree,
   Beside an apple tree did grow.
   And there a boy met his bride to be
   Long, long ago.

Come Rain or Come Shine

from ST. LOUIS WOMAN
Words by Johnny Mercer
Music by Harold Arlen

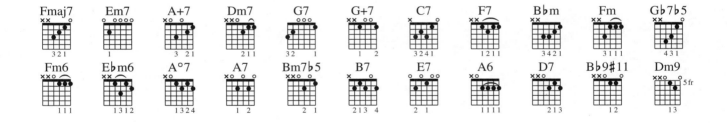

Strum Pattern: 3
Pick Pattern: 3

Verse
Slowly

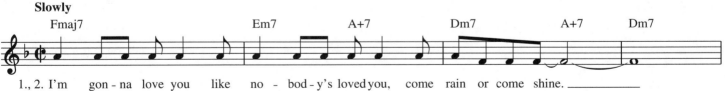

1., 2. I'm gon - na love you like no - bod - y's loved you, come rain or come shine. _____

High as a moun-tain and deep as a riv - er, come rain or come shine. _____

Bridge

I guess when you met me it was just one of those things,

but don't ev-er bet me, 'cause I'm gon-na be true if you let me.

Outro

You're gon-na love me like no-bod-y's loved me, come rain or come shine. _____

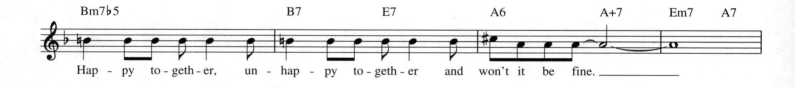

Hap-py to-geth-er, un-hap-py to-geth-er and won't it be fine. _____

Days may be cloud-y or sun-ny, we're in or we're out of the mon-ey, but I'm with you al-ways,

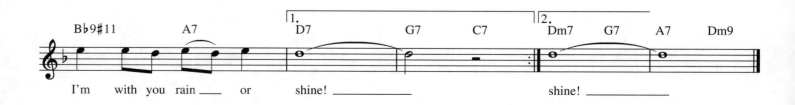

I'm with you rain ___ or shine! _____ shine! _____

Could It Be You

Words and Music by Cole Porter

Strum Pattern: 3, 4
Pick Pattern: 4, 6

Verse

Moderately

A white sea-shore in moon-light im-mersed, a si-lent palm-tree sway-ing;

when out of no-where you sud-den-ly burst, and I found my-self say-ing: _____

Chorus

Could it be you, the one I'm fat-ed for? _ Could it be

you, the love I've wait-ed for? _ For lo, since

you came a-long, _ and kin-dled the song _ in my heart, why both-er pre-

tend-ing? The song _ is un-end-ing. Are you the

dream, I al-ways dream a-bout? _ Are we the

team   I'm   on   the   beam   a - bout? _   Could   be,   these

rev-'ries of mine, _   are   far   too   di - vine _   to   come   true,   or   could   it

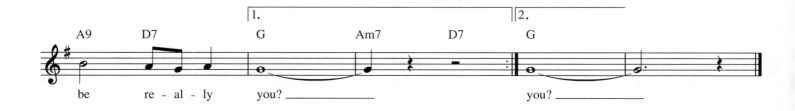

be   re - al - ly   you? _____   you? _____

A Day in the Life of a Fool
(Manhá De Carnaval)
Words by Carl Sigman
Music by Luiz Bonfa

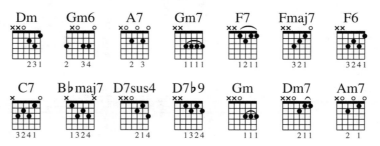

Strum Pattern: 3
Pick Pattern: 3

Verse
Slow Bossa Nova

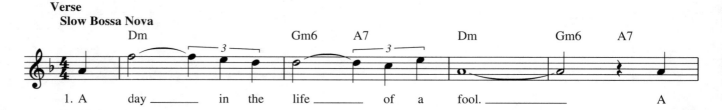

1. A   day _____ in   the   life _____ of   a   fool. _____   A

sad _____ and   a   long, _____ lone - ly   day. _____   I   walk   the

av - e - nue, _____ and hope I'll run in - to _____ the wel - come

sight of you _____ com - ing my way. 2. I

Verse

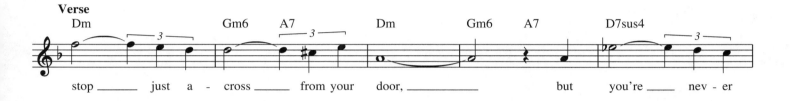

stop _____ just a - cross _____ from your door, _____ but you're _____ nev - er

home _____ an - y - more. _____ So back to my room

and there in the gloom I cry _____ tears of good -

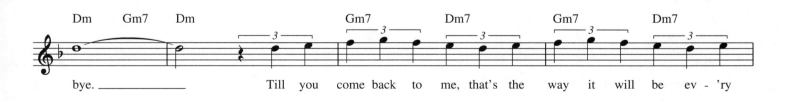

bye. _____ Till you come back to me, that's the way it will be ev - 'ry

day in the life of a fool. _____

Darn That Dream

Lyric by Eddie De Lange
Music by Jimmy Van Heusen

Strum Pattern: 2, 4
Pick Pattern: 1, 6

Verse
Slowly

1. Darn that dream I dream each night, you say you love me and you hold me tight,
2., 3. *See additional lyrics*

but when I a-wake you're out of sight. Oh, darn that dream.

darn that dream. Darn that one track mind of mine, __ it

can't un-der-stand __ that you don't care. __ Just to change the mood I'm in, ___ I'd

wel-come a nice __ old night - mare.

darn that dream.

Additional Lyrics

2. Darn your lips and darn your eyes,
They lift me high above the moonlit skies,
Then I tumble out of paradise.
Oh, darn that dream.

3. Darn that dream and bless it too,
Without that dream, I never would have you,
But it haunts me and it won't come true,
Oh, darn that dream.

Day by Day

Theme from the Paramount Television Series DAY BY DAY
Words and Music by Sammy Cahn, Axel Stordahl and Paul Weston

Strum Pattern: 4, 5
Pick Pattern: 4, 5

Easy Living

Theme from the Paramount Picture EASY LIVING
Words and Music by Leo Robin and Ralph Rainger

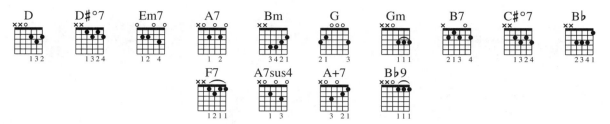

Strum Pattern: 3, 4
Pick Pattern: 3, 6

Verse
Moderately

1., 2. Liv-ing for you, is eas-y liv-ing. It's eas-y to live when you're in love _ and

I'm so in love, there's noth-ing in life ___ but you. _____ I

nev-er re-gret the years I'm giv-ing. They're eas-y to give

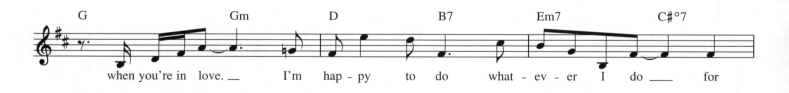

when you're in love. _ I'm hap-py to do what-ev-er I do ___ for

Bridge

you, _____ for you. May-be I'm a fool _ but it's fun. _

___ Peo-ple say you rule me with one _____ wave of your hand. _

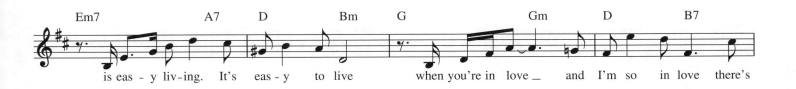

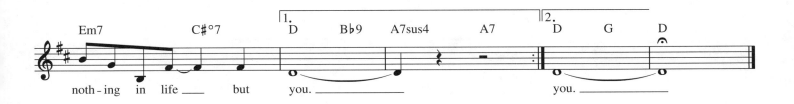

Girl Talk

from the Paramount Picture HARLOW
Words by Bobby Troup
Music by Neal Hefti

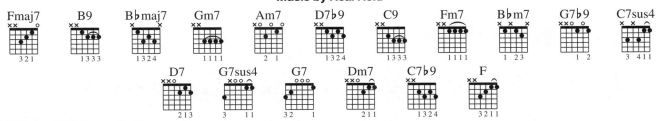

Strum Pattern: 2, 3
Pick Pattern: 3, 6

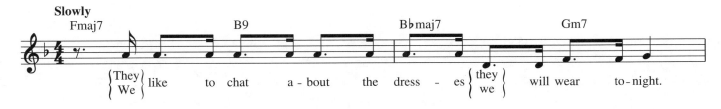

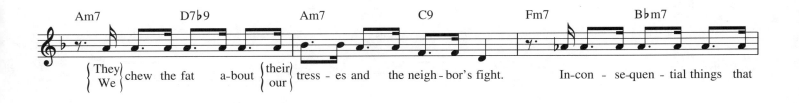

men don't real - ly care to know   be-come es-sen - tial things that wo - men find   so "ap - pro-po".

But that's a dame, {they're / we're} all the same;   it's just a game. {They / We} call   it   girl   talk,

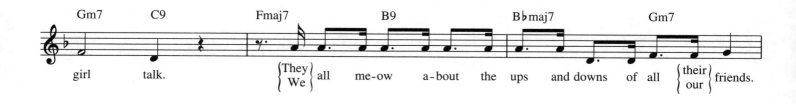

girl   talk.   {They / We} all   me-ow   a-bout   the   ups   and   downs   of   all   {their / our} friends.

The "who",   the "how",   the "why", {they / we} dish the dirt,   it   nev - er ends.   The weak - er sex,   the speak - er

sex {we / you} mor - tal males   be-hold.   But though   we joke   we would - n't trade   you for   a   ton   of gold.

So   ba - by   stay   and   gab a - way,   but hear me say   that   af - ter girl   talk,
It's   all been planned,   so take my hand,   please un - der-stand   the   sweet - est girl   talk

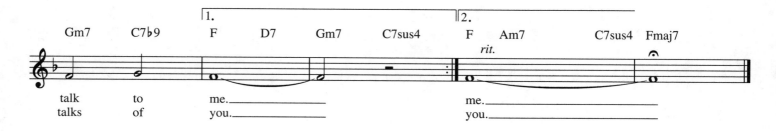

talk   to   me._____   me._____
talks   of   you._____   you._____

Easy to Love (You'd Be So Easy to Love)

from BORN TO DANCE
Words and Music by Cole Porter

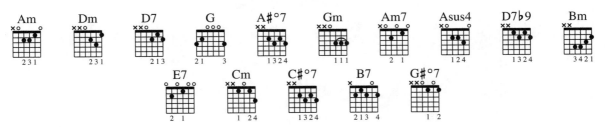

Strum Pattern: 3, 4
Pick Pattern: 1, 6

Moderately

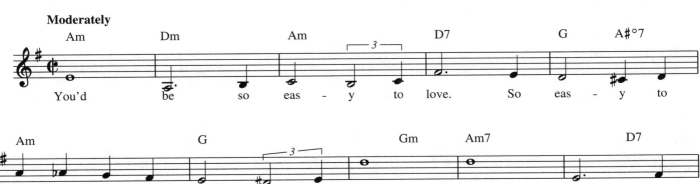

You'd be so eas-y to love. So eas-y to

i-dol-ize, all oth-ers a-bove. So worth the

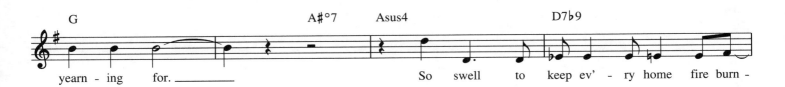

yearn-ing for. _____ So swell to keep ev'-ry home fire burn-

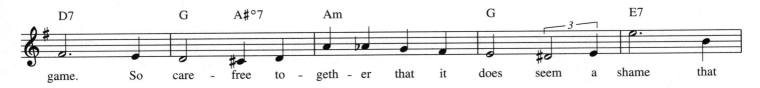

-ing for. _____ We'd be so grand at the

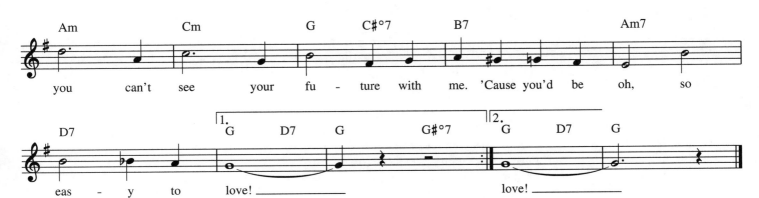

game. So care-free to-geth-er that it does seem a shame that

you can't see your fu-ture with me. 'Cause you'd be oh, so

eas-y to love! _____ love! _____

Falling in Love With Love

from THE BOYS FROM SYRACUSE
Words by Lorenz Hart
Music by Richard Rodgers

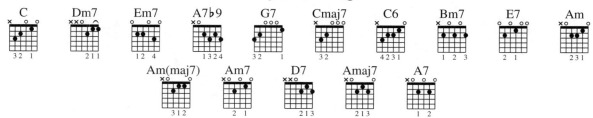

Strum Pattern: 9
Pick Pattern: 9

Additional Lyrics

2. I fell in love with love one night when the moon was full,
   I was unwise with eyes unable to see.
   I fell in love with love, with love everlasting,
   But love fell out with me.

Fly Me to the Moon
(In Other Words)

featured in the Motion Picture ONCE AROUND

Words and Music by Bart Howard

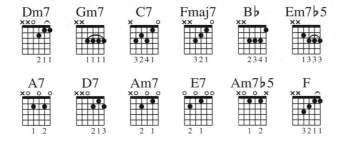

Strum Pattern: 3, 4
Pick Pattern: 3, 4

Georgia on My Mind

Words by Stuart Gorrell
Music by Hoagy Carmichael

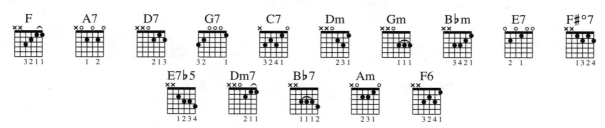

Strum Pattern: 4
Pick Pattern: 6

Verse
Slowly

Mel - o - dies bring mem - o - ries that lin - ger in my

heart. _____ Make me think of Geor - gia, why

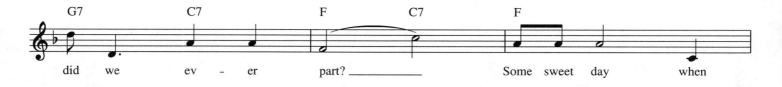

did we ev - er part? _____ Some sweet day when

blos - soms fall and all the world's a song, _____

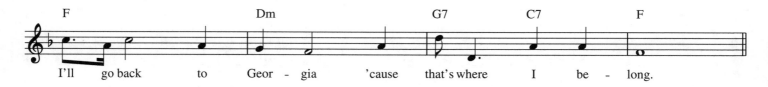

I'll go back to Geor - gia 'cause that's where I be - long.

Chorus

Geor - gia, _____ Geor - gia, _____ the whole day

The Gift!
(Recado Bossa Nova)

Music by Djalma Ferreira
Original Lyric by Luiz Antonio
English Lyric by Paul Francis Webster

Strum Pattern: 2, 5
Pick Pattern: 1, 4

Additional Lyrics

2., 3. Voce dei xou semquerer dei xou
Uma sauda dee nor meem seu lugar
De pois no's dois cada qual a mer ce
Do seu desti no voce seu mim eu sem voce.

God Bless' the Child

featured in the Motion Picture LADY SINGS THE BLUES
Words and Music by Arthur Herzog Jr. and Billie Holiday

Strum Pattern: 4
Pick Pattern: 5

Additional Lyrics

2. Yes, the strong gets more, while the weak ones fade,
   Empty pockets don't ever make the grade.
   Mama may have, Papa may have,
   But God bless' the child that's got his own!
   That's got his own.

3. Rich relations give, crust of bread, and such,
   You can help yourself, but don't take too much!
   Mama may have, Papa may have,
   But God bless' the child that's got his own!
   That's got his own.

Harlem Nocturne

Music by Earle Hagen
Words by Dick Rogers

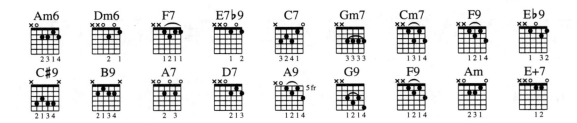

Strum Pattern: 2, 4
Pick Pattern: 1, 3

Verse

Slowly

1. Deep mu - sic fills the night, _____ deep in the heart of Har -
2. *See Additional Lyrics*

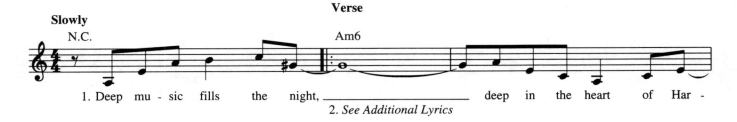

lem. _____ And tho' the stars are bright, _____

___ the dark - ness is taun - ting me. _____ Oh! What a sad re - frain, _

1.

2.

Bridge

_____ The mel - o - dy clings ___ a -
See Additional Lyrics

round my heart strings. _ It won't let me go ___ when I'm lone - ly, _____ I

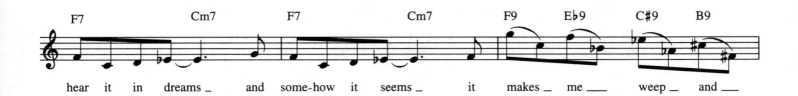

hear it in dreams _ and some-how it seems _ it makes _ me _ weep _ and _

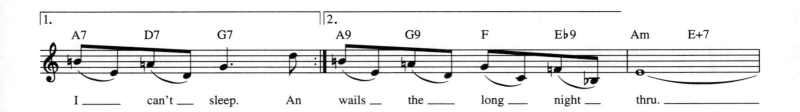

I _ can't _ sleep. An wails _ the _ long _ night _ thru. _

Outro

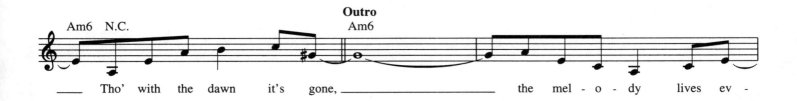

_ Tho' with the dawn it's gone, _ the mel - o - dy lives ev -

er _ for lone - ly hearts to learn _

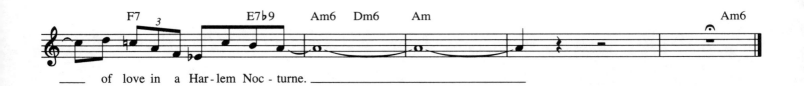

_ of love in a Har - lem Noc - turne. _

Additional Lyrics

2. Oh! What a sad refrain,
A nocturne born in Harlem.
That melancholy strain
Forever is haunting me.

Bridge An indigo tune, it sings to the moon
The lonesome refrain of a lover.
The melody sighs, it laughs and it cries,
A moan in blue that wails the long night thru.

Have You Met Miss Jones?

from I'D RATHER BE RIGHT
Words by Lorenz Hart
Music by Richard Rodgers

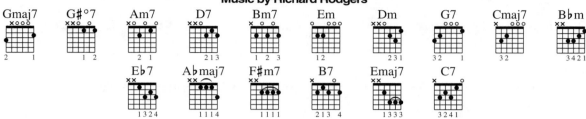

Strum Pattern: 4
Pick Pattern: 5

Verse
Moderate Swing

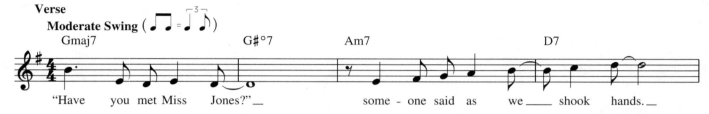

"Have you met Miss Jones?" ___ some - one said as we ___ shook hands. ___

She was just Miss Jones ___ to me. ___

Then I said, "Miss Jones, ___ you're a girl who un - der - stands, ___

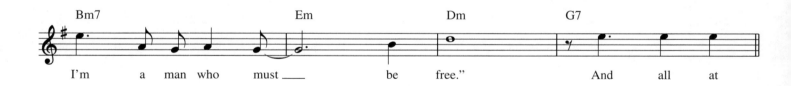

I'm a man who must ___ be free." And all at

Bridge

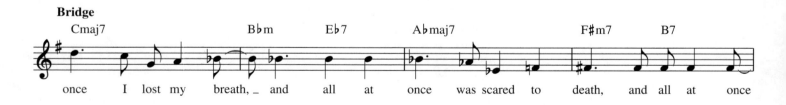

once I lost my breath, ___ and all at once was scared to death, and all at once

___ I owned the earth and sky! ___

Outro

Gmaj7 ... G#°7 ... Am7

Now I've met Miss Jones, ___ and we'll keep on meet-

D7 ... C7 ... Bm7 ... E7 ... Am7 ... D7

-ing till we die, ___ Miss Jones and

1. Gmaj7 Em Am7 D7 2. Gmaj7

I. I. ___

Hello, Young Lovers

from THE KING AND I

Lyrics by Oscar Hammerstein II
Music by Richard Rodgers

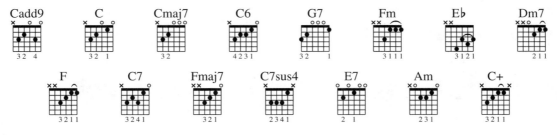

Cadd9 C Cmaj7 C6 G7 Fm E♭ Dm7

F C7 Fmaj7 C7sus4 E7 Am C+

Strum Pattern: 7
Pick Pattern: 9

Verse

Moderately

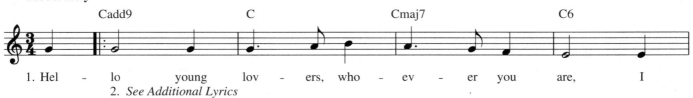

Cadd9 ... C ... Cmaj7 ... C6

1. Hel - lo young lov - ers, who - ev - er you are, I
2. *See Additional Lyrics*

Cmaj7 ... C6 ... G7 ... Fm

hope your trou - bles are few. ___ All my good

G7 ... E♭ ... G7 ... Dm7 ... G7

wish - es go with you to - night. I've been in love like

Additional Lyrics

2. Be brave young lovers and follow your star,
    Be brave and faithful and true.
    Cling very close to each other tonight.
    I've been in love like you.

How Deep Is the Ocean
(How High Is the Sky)

Words and Music by Irving Berlin

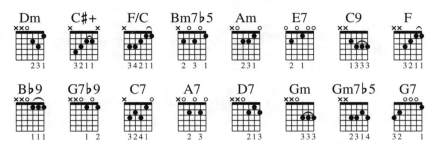

Strum Pattern: 4
Pick Pattern: 1

Verse
Moderately

How much do I love you? I'll tell you no lie,

how deep is the o-cean, how high is the sky? How man-y

times a day ___ do I think of you? ___ How man-y ros - es are

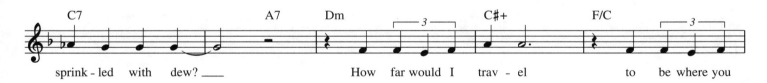

sprink-led with dew? ___ How far would I trav-el to be where you

are? How far is the jour-ney from here to a star?

And if I ev-er lost you, how much would I cry?

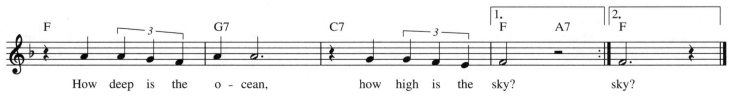

How deep is the o-cean, how high is the sky? sky?

Honeysuckle Rose

from AIN'T MISBEHAVIN'
Words by Andy Razaf
Music by Thomas "Fats" Waller

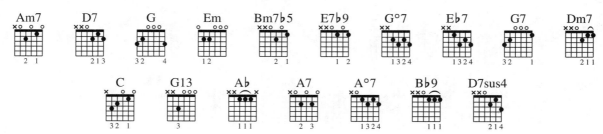

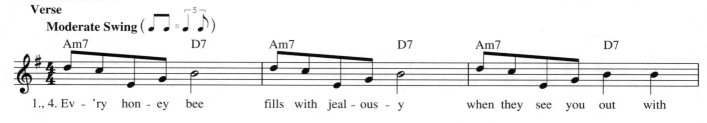

Strum Pattern: 4
Pick Pattern: 5

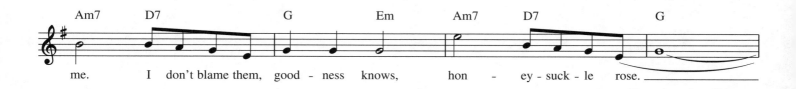

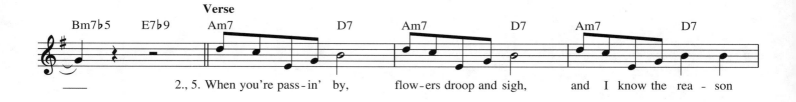

you just have to touch my cup. ___ You're my sug - ar,

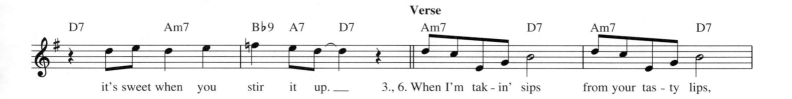

Verse

it's sweet when you stir it up. ___ 3., 6. When I'm tak - in' sips from your tas - ty lips,

seems the hon - ey fair - ly drips. You're con - fec - tion, good - ness knows, hon - ey - suck - le

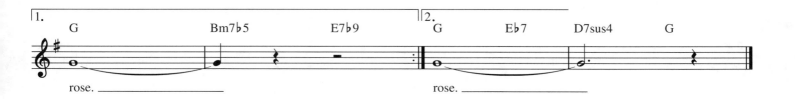

1.
rose. _____

2.
rose. _____

Verse

it's sweet when you stir it up. ___ 3., 6. When I'm tak - in' sips

from your tas - ty lips, seems the hon - ey fair - ly drips. You're con - fec - tion,

good - ness knows, hon - ey - suck - le

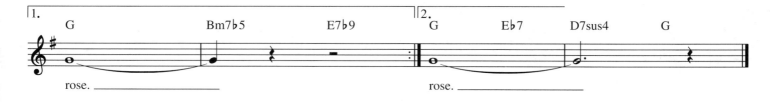

1.
rose. _____

2.
rose. _____

How High the Moon

from TWO FOR THE SHOW

Words by Nancy Hamilton

Music by Morgan Lewis

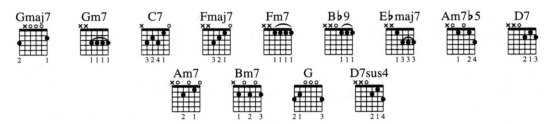

Strum Pattern: 4
Pick Pattern: 5

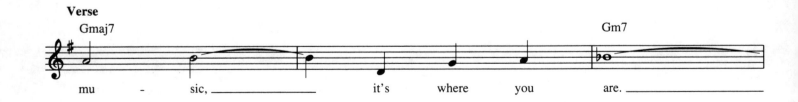

far! _____ The dark - est night would shine if you would come _ to me

soon. _____ Un - til you will, how still my heart, how high the

moon! _____   3. Some - where there's   moon! _____

I Can't Get Started With You

from ZIEGFELD FOLLIES
Words by Ira Gershwin
Music by Vernon Duke

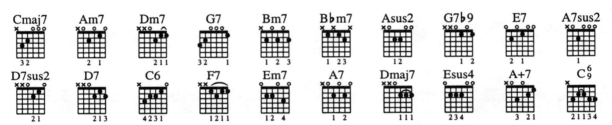

Strum Pattern: 3, 4
Pick Pattern: 1, 6

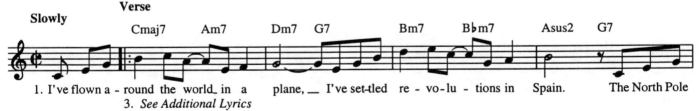

1. I've flown a - round the world_ in a plane, _ I've set-tled re - vo-lu - tions in Spain. The North Pole
3. *See Additional Lyrics*

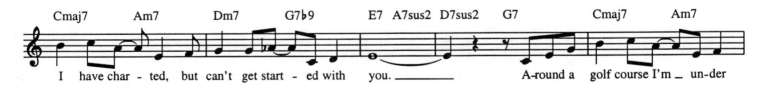

I have char - ted, but can't get start - ed with you. _____ A-round a golf course I'm _ un - der

par, _____ and all the mov - ies want _ me to star. I've got a house, a show _ place, but

I get no — place with you. You're so su-preme, lyr-ics I write — of you,
See Additional Lyrics

scheme just for a sight — of you. Dream both day and night — of you

and what good does it do? 2. In nine-teen twen-ty-nine — I sold short, ——— in Eng-land
4. *See Additional Lyrics*

I'm pre-sent — ed at court. But you've got me down-heart — ed 'cause I

can't get start — ed with you. 3. I do a you. ———————

Additional Lyrics

3. I do a hundred yards in ten flat,
   The Prince of Wales has copied my hat.
   With queens I've a la carted,
   But can't get started with you.
   The leading tailors follow my styles,
   And toothpaste ads all feature my smiles.
   The Astorbilts I visit, but say,
   What is it with you?

Bridge When we first met, how you elated me!
   Pet, you devastated me!
   Yet, now you've deflated me
   Till you're my Waterloo.

4. I've sold my kisses at a bazaar,
   And after me they've named a cigar.
   But lately how I've smarted,
   'Cause I can't get started with you.

I Could Write a Book

from PAL JOEY

Words by Lorenz Hart
Music by Richard Rodgers

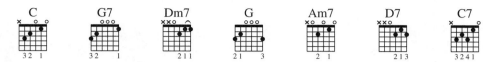

Strum Pattern: 3
Pick Pattern: 3

I Didn't Know What Time It Was

from TOO MANY GIRLS

Words by Lorenz Hart
Music by Richard Rodgers

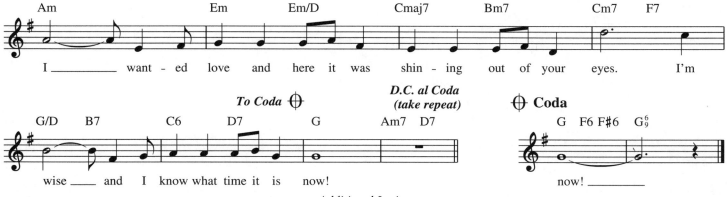

Additional Lyrics

2., 4. I didn't know what day it was;
You held my hand.
Warm like the month of May it was
And I'll say it was grand.

I Get Along Without You Very Well
(Except Sometimes)

Words and Music by Hoagy Carmichael
Inspired by a poem written by J.B. Thompson

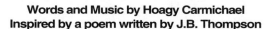

Strum Pattern: 3, 4
Pick Pattern: 3

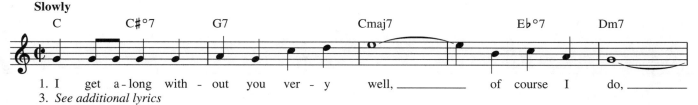

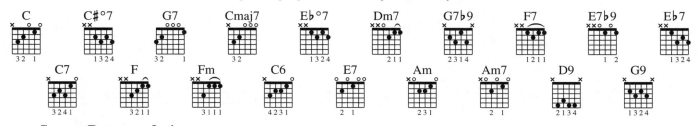

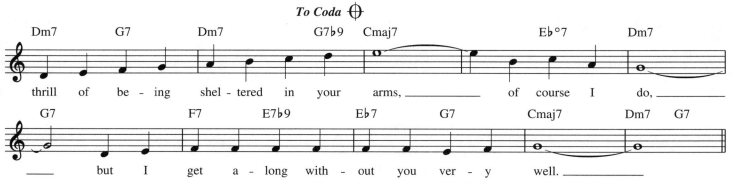

Verse

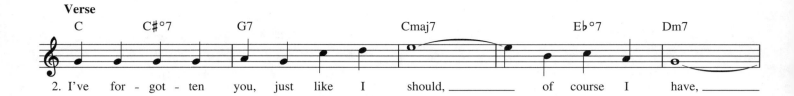

2. I've for - got - ten you, just like I should, _____ of course I have, _____

_____ ex - cept to hear your name _____ or some - one's laugh that is the same but

Bridge

I've for - got - ten you just like I should. _____ What a guy! _____ What a

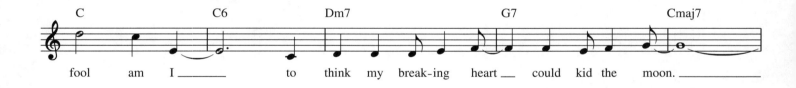

fool am I _____ to think my break - ing heart __ could kid the moon. _____

_____ What's in store? _____ Should I 'phone once more? __ No, it's

D.C. al Coda   **Coda**

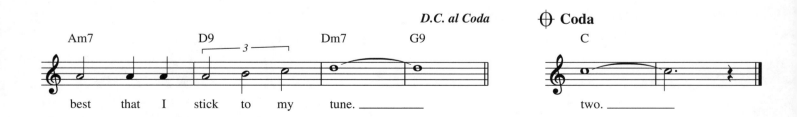

best that I stick to my tune. _____   two. _____

Additional Lyrics

3. I get along without you very well,
Of course I do, except perhaps in spring,
But I should never think of spring
For that would surely break my heart in two.

I Don't Stand a Ghost of a Chance

Words by Bing Crosby and Ned Washington
Music by Victor Young

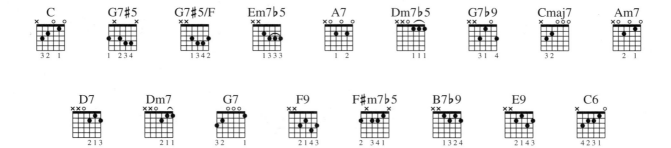

Strum Pattern: 3, 4
Pick Pattern: 5, 6

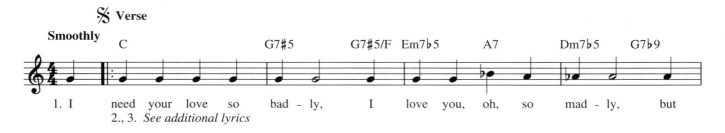

1. I need your love so bad-ly, I love you, oh, so mad-ly, but
2., 3. *See additional lyrics*

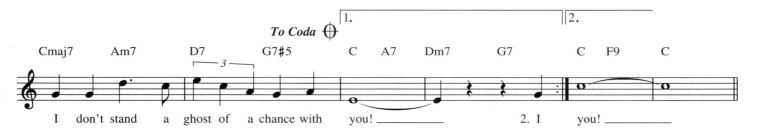

I don't stand a ghost of a chance with you! _____ 2. I _____ you! _____

Bridge

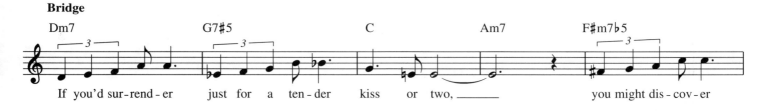

If you'd sur-rend-er just for a ten-der kiss or two, _____ you might dis-cov-er

that I'm the lov-er meant for you, and I'd be true. 3. But   you! _____

Additional Lyrics

2. I thought at last I'd found you,
   But other loves surround you, and
   I don't stand a ghost of a chance with you!

3. But what's the good of scheming,
   I know I must be dreaming, for
   I don't stand a ghost of a chance with you!

I Hear a Rhapsody

By George Frajos, Jack Baker and Dick Gasparre

Strum Pattern: 3, 4
Pick Pattern: 3, 5

Additional Lyrics

2. And when your sparkling eyes are smiling at me,
   Then soft through the starlit skies,
   I hear a rhapsody.

3. My darling, hold me tight and whisper to me,
   Then soft through a starry night,
   I hear a rhapsody.

I Hear Music
from the Paramount Picture DANCING ON A DIME
Words by Frank Loesser
Music by Burton Lane

Strum Pattern: 3, 4
Pick Pattern: 1, 2

Additional Lyrics

2., 4. Sure that's music, mighty fine music,
The singing of a sparrow in the sky,
The perking of the coffee right near by.

I Remember You

from the Paramount Picture THE FLEET'S IN
Words by Johnny Mercer
Music by Victor Schertzinger

Strum Pattern: 4
Pick Pattern: 5

Additional Lyrics

2. I remember you.
   You're the one who said:
   "I love you too."
   I do. Didn't you know?

I'm Beginning to See the Light

Words and Music by Don George, Johnny Hodges, Duke Ellington and Harry James

Strum Pattern: 2, 4
Pick Pattern: 1, 2

𝄋 **Verse**

Moderate Swing

1. I (3.) nev-er cared much for moon-lit skies, __ I nev-er wink back at fi - re - flies; __ but
2., 4. *See additional lyrics*

now that the stars are in your eyes, __ I'm be - gin-ning to see the light. __ 2., 4. I __

Bridge

Used to ram - ble thru the park, __ shad - ow - box - ing in the dark. __

Then you came and caused a spark, __ that's a four - a - larm fi - re now. __ I

Outro

nev - er made love by lan - tern shine, __ I nev - er saw rain - bows in my wine; __ but

To Coda ⊕   ***D.S. al Coda*** (take repeat)   ⊕ **Coda**

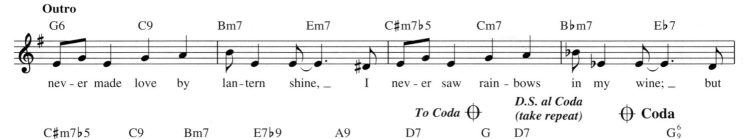

now that your lips are burn - ing mine, __ I'm be - gin - ning to see the light. __ 3. I __

Additional Lyrics

2., 4. I never went in for after glow,
Or candlelight on the mistletoe;
But now when you turn the lamp down low
I'm beginning to see the light.

I've Got the World on a String

Lyric by Ted Koehler
Music by Harold Arlen

Strum Pattern: 2, 4
Pick Pattern: 1, 2

Additional Lyrics

2. I've got a song that I sing,
   I can make the rain go, anytime I move my finger.
   Lucky me, can't you see, I'm in love?

I've Got You Under My Skin

from BORN TO DANCE
Words and Music by Cole Porter

peats and re-peats in my ear: ____ "Don't you know, lit-tle fool, ____ you nev-er can win, ____

____ use your men-tal - i-ty, ____ wake up to re-al - i-ty." ____ But each

time I do, just the thought of you makes me stop be-fore I be - gin, 'cause I've got you ____

____ un - der my skin. ____ 2. I've skin.

I've Grown Accustomed to Her Face

from MY FAIR LADY

Words by Alan Jay Lerner
Music by Frederick Loewe

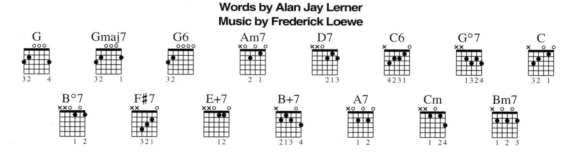

Strum Pattern: 4
Pick Pattern: 4

Verse

Moderately Slow

1. I've grown ac - cus-tomed to her face. ____ She al-most makes the day be - gin.
2. *See Additional Lyrics*

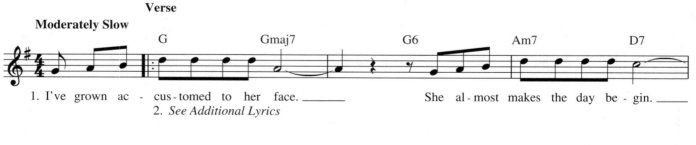

____ I've grown ac - cus-tomed to the tune she whist - les night and noon. Her

smiles, her frowns, her ups, her downs are sec-ond na-ture to me now. _____ Like breath-ing

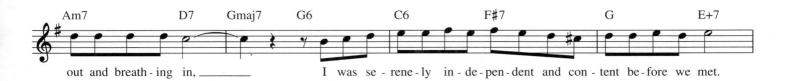

out and breath-ing in, _____ I was se-rene-ly in-de-pen-dent and con-tent be-fore we met.

Chorus

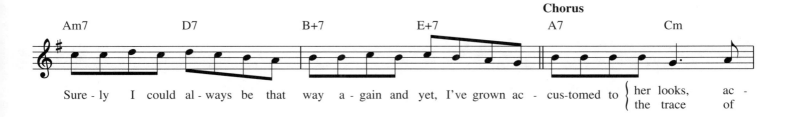

Sure-ly I could al-ways be that way a-gain and yet, I've grown ac-cus-tomed to { her looks, ac-
the trace of

cus-tomed to her voice,}
some-thing in the air,}   ac-cus-tomed to her face.   2. I've grown ac-face.

Additional Lyrics

2. I've grown accustomed to her face.
   She makes the day begin.
   I've gotten used to hear her say,
   "Good morning", ev'ry day.
   Her joys, her woes,
   Her highs, her lows are second nature to me now.
   Like breathing out and breathing in,
   I'm very grateful she's a woman
   And so easy to forget
   Rather like a habit one can always break, and yet,

If I Should Lose You

from the Paramount Picture ROSE OF THE RANCHO
Words and Music by Leo Robin and Ralph Rainger

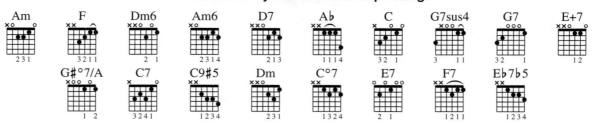

Strum Pattern: 3
Pick Pattern: 4

Verse
Moderately

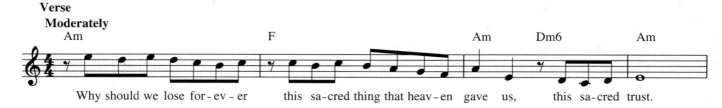

Why should we lose for-ev-er this sa-cred thing that heav-en gave us, this sa-cred trust.

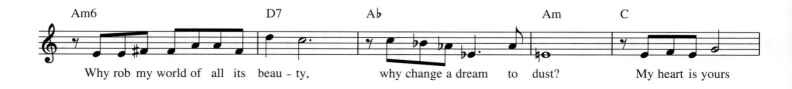

Why rob my world of all its beau-ty, why change a dream to dust? My heart is yours

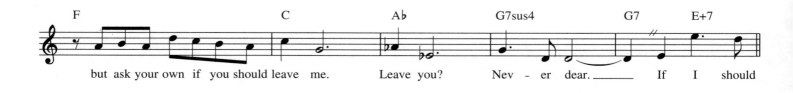

but ask your own if you should leave me. Leave you? Nev-er dear. _____ If I should

Chorus

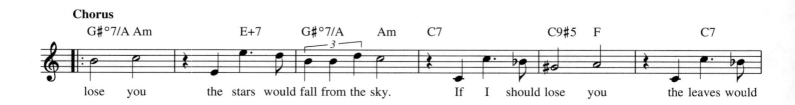

lose you the stars would fall from the sky. If I should lose you the leaves would

with-er and die. The birds in May-time _____ would sing a mourn-ful re-frain and I would

wan-der a-round hat-ing the sound of rain. _____ With you be - side me the rose would

bloom in the snow. With you be - side me no winds of win - ter would blow.

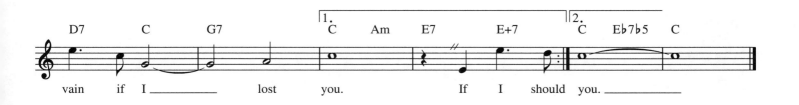

I gave you my love _____ and I was liv-ing a dream, but liv-ing would seem in

vain if I _____ lost you. If I should you. _____

In a Sentimental Mood

Words and Music by Duke Ellington, Irving Mills and Manny Kurtz

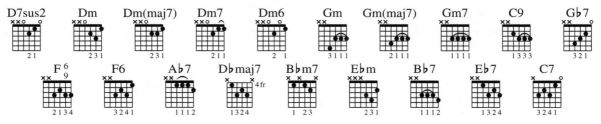

Strum Pattern: 2
Pick Pattern: 2

Verse

Moderately

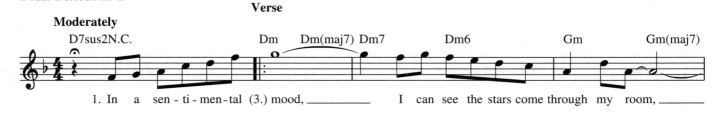

1. In a sen - ti - men - tal (3.) mood, _____ I can see the stars come through my room, _____

_____ while your lov - ing at - ti - tude _____ is like a flame that lights the

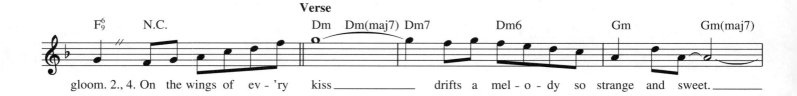

Verse

gloom. 2., 4. On the wings of ev - 'ry kiss _____ drifts a mel - o - dy so strange and sweet. _____

_____ In this sen - ti - men - tal bliss _____ you make my par - a - dise com - plete.

Bridge

Rose pet - als seem to fall, it's all like a dream to call you mine.

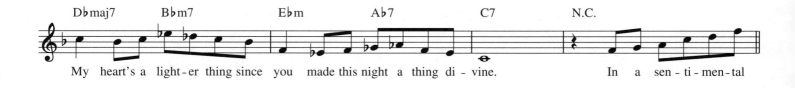

My heart's a light - er thing since you made this night a thing di - vine. In a sen - ti - men - tal

Outro

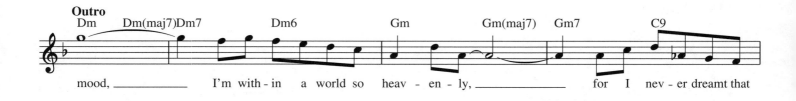

mood, _____ I'm with - in a world so heav - en - ly, _____ for I nev - er dreamt that

you'd _____ be lov - ing sen - ti - men - tal me. 3. In a sen - ti - men - tal me.

Imagination

Words by Johnny Burke
Music by Jimmy Van Heusen

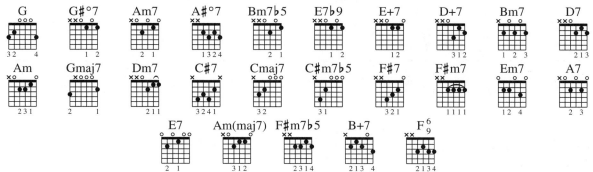

Strum Pattern: 3, 4
Pick Pattern: 3, 6

77

In a Mellow Tone

Words by Milt Gabler
Music by Duke Ellington

Strum Pattern: 2, 5
Pick Pattern: 4, 5

In the Wee Small Hours of the Morning

Words by Bob Hilliard
Music by David Mann

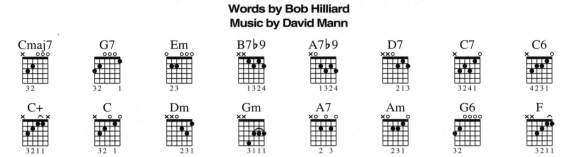

Strum Pattern: 4
Pick Pattern: 4

Indiana
(Back Home Again in Indiana)

Words by Ballard MacDonald
Music by James F. Hanley

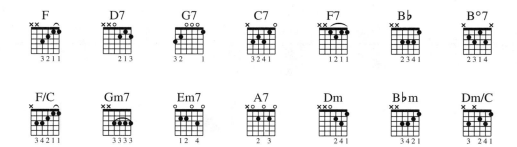

Strum Pattern: 2, 4
Pick Pattern: 1, 3

Back home a - gain _____ in In - di - an - a, _____ and it

seems that I can see _____ the gleam - ing can - dle - light _____ still

shin - ing bright _____ through the syc - a - mores _____ for me. _____

_____ The new mown hay _____ sends all it's fra - grance _____ from the fields I

used to roam; _____ when I dream a - bout the moon - light on the

Wa - bash, _____ then I long for my In - di - an - a home. _____

It Could Happen to You

from the Paramount Picture AND THE ANGELS SING
Words by Johnny Burke
Music by James Van Heusen

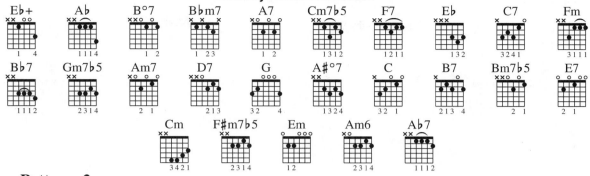

Strum Pattern: 2
Pick Pattern: 2

Verse
Slowly

Do you be - lieve in charms and spells, in mys - tic words and

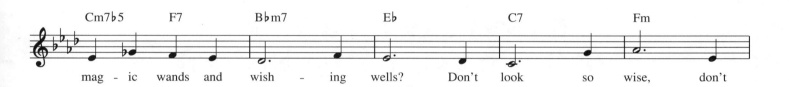

mag - ic wands and wish - ing wells? Don't look so wise, don't

show your scorn; watch your - self, I warn you.

Chorus

Hide your heart from sight, lock your dreams at night. It could

hap - pen to you. _____ Don't count stars or you might stum - ble. _____

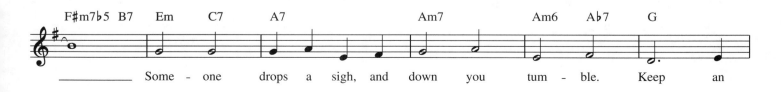

_____ Some - one drops a sigh, and down you tum - ble. Keep an

eye on spring, run when church bells ring. It could hap - pen to

you. _____ All I did was won - der how your arms would be

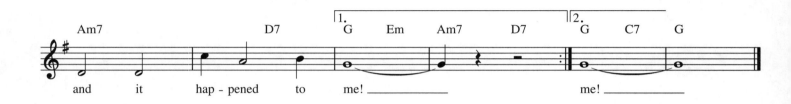

and it hap - pened to me! _____ me! _____

It Don't Mean a Thing
(If It Ain't Got That Swing)

from SOPHISTICATED LADIES
Words and Music by Duke Ellington and Irving Mills

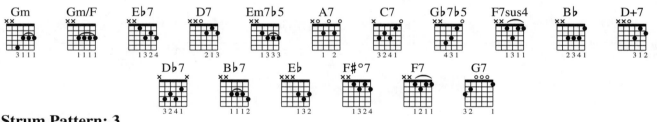

Strum Pattern: 3
Pick Pattern: 4

Verse
Lively

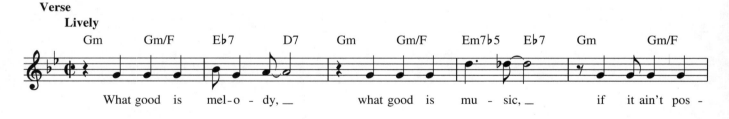

What good is mel - o - dy, __ what good is mu - sic, __ if it ain't pos -

ses - sin' some - thing sweet? _____ It ain't the mel - o - dy, __ it ain't the

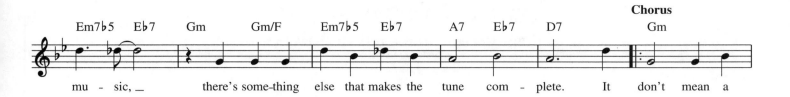

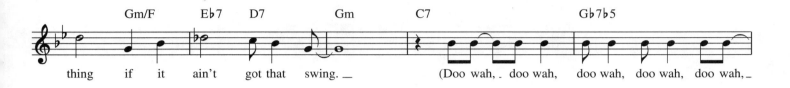

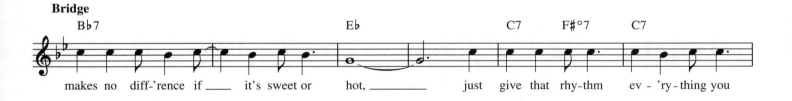

Bridge

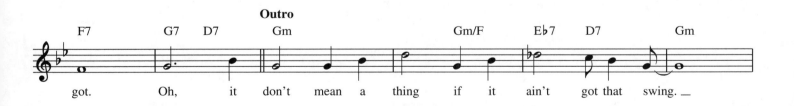

Outro

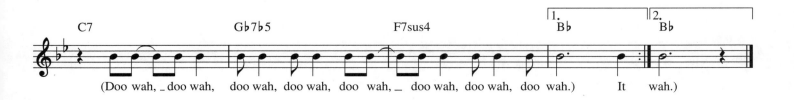

83

Isn't It Romantic?

from the Paramount Picture LOVE ME TONIGHT
Words by Lorenz Hart
Music by Richard Rodgers

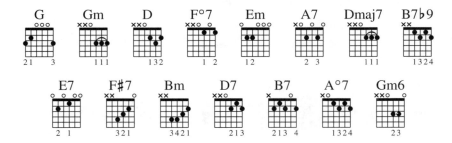

G   Gm   D   F°7   Em   A7   Dmaj7   B7♭9

E7   F#7   Bm   D7   B7   A°7   Gm6

Strum Pattern: 4, 5
Pick Pattern: 4, 5

Verse

Slowly

I've nev-er met you, yet nev-er doubt, dear, I can't for-
2. *See Additional Lyrics*

get you, I've thought you out, dear. I know your pro-file and I know the way you

kiss just the thing I miss on a night like this. If dreams are

made of im-ag-i-na-tion, I'm not a-fraid of my own cre-

a-tion. With all my heart, my heart is here for you to take. Why should I

Chorus

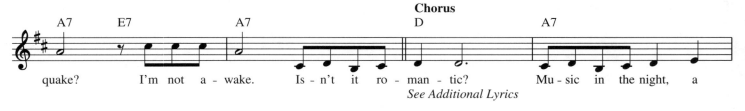

quake? I'm not a-wake. Is-n't it ro-man-tic? Mu-sic in the night, a
See Additional Lyrics

dream that can be heard. Is-n't it ro-man-tic? Mov-ing shad-ows write the

Additional Lyrics

2. My face is glowing, I'm energetic, the art of sewing, I found poetic.
My needle punctuates the rhythm of romance! I don't give a stitch if I don't get rich.
A custom tailor who has no custom, is like a sailor, no one will trust 'em.
But there is magic in the music of my shears; I shed no tears. Lend me your ears!

Chorus Isn't it romantic? Soon I will have found some girl that I adore.
Isn't it romantic? While I sit around, my love can scrub the floor.
She'll kiss me ev'ry hour, or she'll get the sack.
And when I take a shower she can scrub my back.
Isn't it romantic? On a moonlight night she'll cook me onion soup.
Kiddies are romantic, and if we don't fight, we soon will have a troop!
We'll help the population, it's a duty that we owe to dear old France.
Isn't it romance?

It Might As Well Be Spring

from STATE FAIR
Lyrics by Oscar Hammerstein II
Music by Richard Rodgers

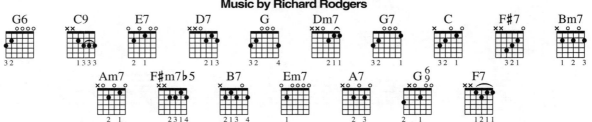

Strum Pattern: 2, 3
Pick Pattern: 3, 4

Verse
Moderately

1. I'm as rest-less as a wil-low in a wind-storm, I'm as jump-y as a pup-pet on a
2. *See Additional Lyrics*

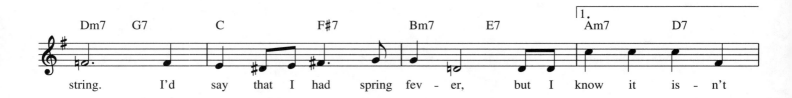

string. I'd say that I had spring fev-er, but I know it is-n't

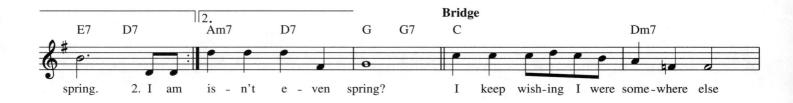

spring. 2. I am is-n't e-ven spring? I keep wish-ing I were some-where else

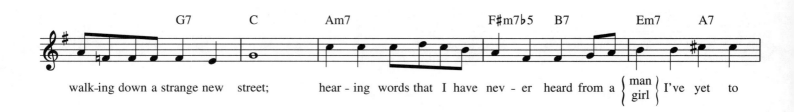

walk-ing down a strange new street; hear-ing words that I have nev-er heard from a { man / girl } I've yet to

Outro

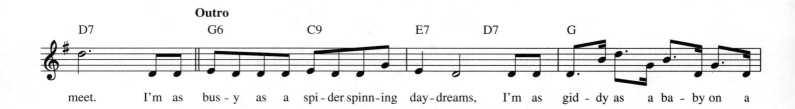

meet. I'm as bus-y as a spi-der spinn-ing day-dreams, I'm as gid-dy as a ba-by on a

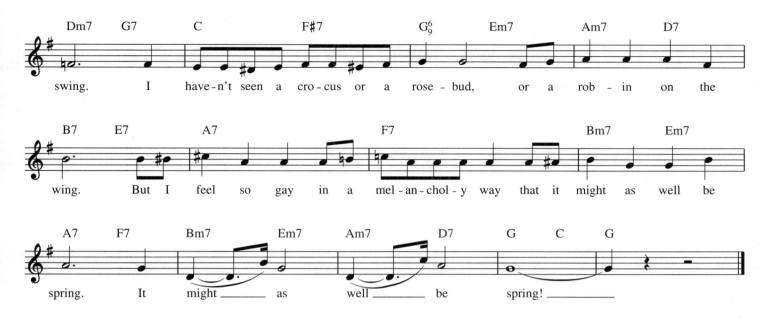

swing. I have-n't seen a cro-cus or a rose-bud, or a rob-in on the

wing. But I feel so gay in a mel-an-chol-y way that it might as well be

spring. It might _____ as well _____ be spring! _____

Additional Lyrics

2. I am starry-eyed and vaguely discontented,
   Like a nightingale without a song to sing.
   Oh, why should I have spring fever,
   When it is'nt even spring?

The Lady Is a Tramp

from BABES IN ARMS
Words by Lorenz Hart
Music by Richard Rodgers

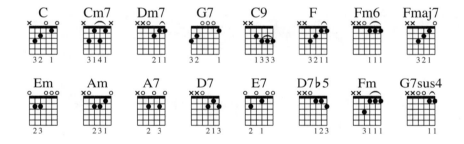

Strum Pattern: 2, 3
Pick Pattern: 3, 4

Verse
Moderately

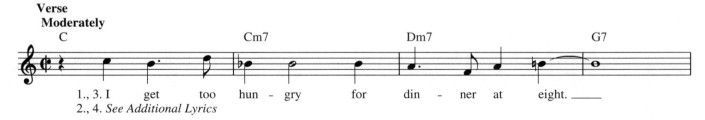

1., 3. I get too hun-gry for din-ner at eight. _____
2., 4. *See Additional Lyrics*

I like the thea-tre but nev-er come late. _____ I nev-er

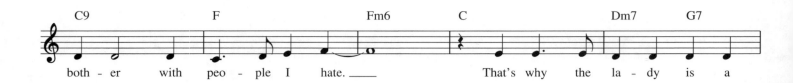
both - er with peo - ple I hate. _____ That's why the la - dy is a

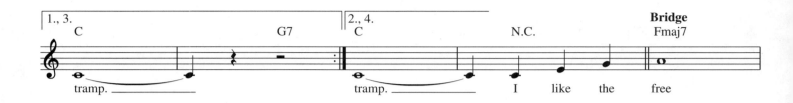
1., 3.
C   G7   **2., 4.**
C   N.C.   **Bridge**
                                                        Fmaj7
tramp. _____   tramp. _____ I like the free

G7   Em   Am   Dm7   G7
fresh   wind   in   my   hair, _____   life   with - out   care. _____

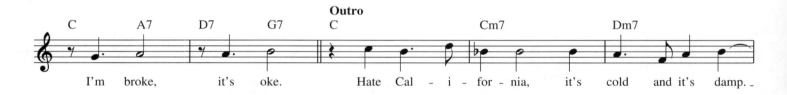
Outro
C   A7   D7   G7   C   Cm7   Dm7
I'm   broke,   it's   oke.   Hate   Cal - i - for - nia,   it's   cold   and it's   damp. _

To Coda ⊕   **_D.C. al Coda_**
(take repeat)

E7   Am   D7   G7   C   Am   Dm7   G7
___   That's   why   the   la - dy   is   a   tramp. _____

⊕ **_Coda_**

D7   D7♭5   G7
la - dy   is   a

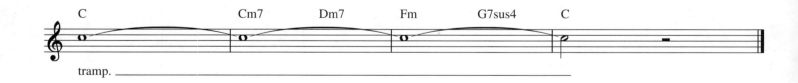
C   Cm7   Dm7   Fm   G7sus4   C
tramp. _____

Additional Lyrics

2., 4. I don't like crap games with Barons and Earls,
Won't go to Harlem in ermine and pearls.
Won't dish the dirt with the rest of the girls,
That's why the lady is a tramp.

Like Someone in Love

Words by Johnny Burke
Music by Jimmy Van Heusen

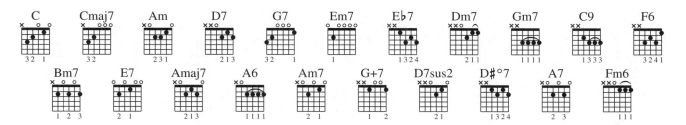

Strum Pattern: 3, 4
Pick Pattern: 3, 6

Lover

from the Paramount Picture LOVE ME TONIGHT

Words by Lorenz Hart
Music by Richard Rodgers

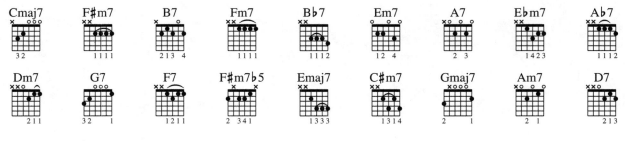

Strum Pattern: 2, 6
Pick Pattern: 4

Verse

Brightly

1. Lov - er, _____ when I'm near you _____ and I hear you _____ speak my
2., 3. *See additional lyrics*

name, _____ soft - ly _____ in my ear, you _____ breathe a

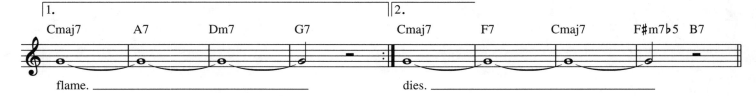

flame. _____ dies. _____

Bridge

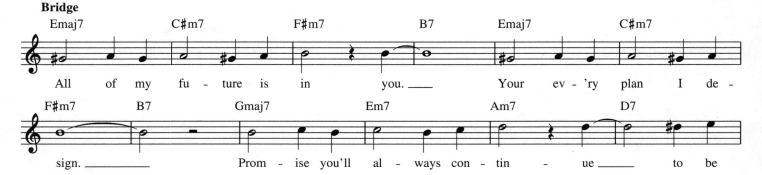

All of my fu - ture is in you. _____ Your ev - 'ry plan I de -

sign. _____ Prom - ise you'll al - ways con - tin - ue _____ to be

D.C. al Coda ⊕ **Coda**

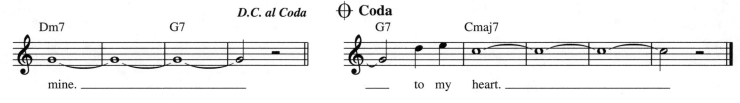

mine. _____ _____ to my heart. _____

Additional Lyrics

2. Lover, when we're dancing
   Keep on glancing in my eyes,
   Till love's own entrancing music dies.

3. Lover, please be tender,
   When your tender fears depart,
   Lover, I surrender to my heart.

Misty

Words by Johnny Burke
Music by Erroll Garner

Strum Pattern: 4
Pick Pattern: 5

Additional Lyrics

2. Walk my way,
   And a thousand violins begin to play,
   Or it might be the sound of your hello,
   That music I hear,
   I get misty the moment you're near.

3. On my own,
   Would I wander through this wonderland alone,
   Never knowing my right foot from my left,
   My hat from my glove?
   I'm too misty and too much in love.

Mood Indigo

from SOPHISTICATED LADIES
Words and Music by Duke Ellington, Irving Mills and Albany Bigard

Moon River

from the Paramount Picture BREAKFAST AT TIFFANY'S
Words by Johnny Mercer
Music by Henry Mancini

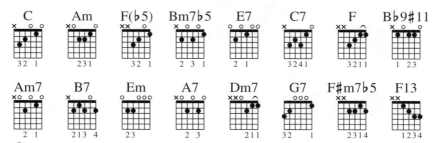

Strum Pattern: 8
Pick Pattern: 8

Slowly

Moon Riv - er, wid - er than a mile: I'm cross - in' you in

style some day. Old dream - mak - er, you heart -

break - er, wher - ev - er you're go - in', I'm go - in' your way. Two

drift - ers, off to see the world. There's such a lot of world to see.

We're af - ter the same rain - bow's end.

wait - in' 'round the bend, my Huck - le - ber - ry friend, Moon

Riv - er and me. me.

More
(Ti Guarderó Nel Cuore)

from the film MONDO CANE

Music by Nino Oliviero and Riz Ortolani
Italian Lyrics by Marcello Ciorciolini
English Lyrics by Norman Newell

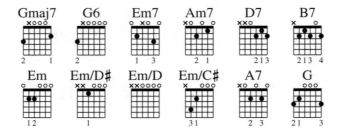

Strum Pattern: 3, 4
Pick Pattern: 1, 3

Verse
Smoothly

More than the great-est love the world has known; this is the
More than the sim-ple words I try to say; I on-ly

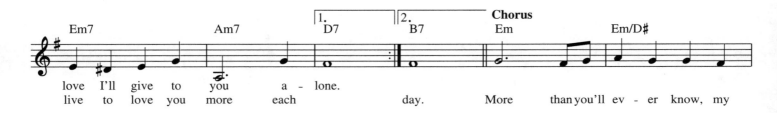

love I'll give to you a - lone.
live to love you more each day. More than you'll ev - er know, my

arms long to hold you so, my life will be in your keep - ing wak - ing, sleep - ing,

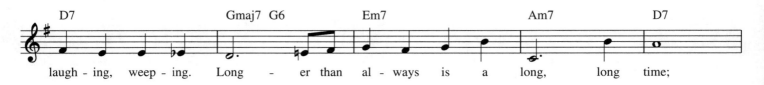

laugh - ing, weep - ing. Long - er than al - ways is a long, long time;

but far be - yond for - ev - er you'll be mine. I know I nev - er lived be -

fore and my heart is ver - y sure no one else could love you more. _____

My Favorite Things

from THE SOUND OF MUSIC
Lyrics by Oscar Hammerstein II
Music by Richard Rodgers

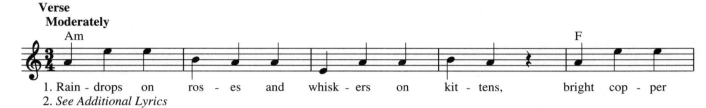

Strum Pattern: 7
Pick Pattern: 8

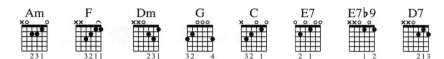

Verse
Moderately

1. Rain - drops on ros - es and whisk - ers on kit - tens, bright cop - per
2. *See Additional Lyrics*

ket - tles and warm wool - en mit - tens, brown pa - per pack - ag - es

tied up with strings, these are a few of my fa - vor - ite things.

fa - vor - ite things. When the dog bites, when the

bee stings, when I'm feel - ing sad, _____ I

sim - ply re - mem - ber my fa - vor - ite things and then I don't

feel _____ so bad. _____

Additional Lyrics

2. Cream colored ponies and crisp apple strudels,
   Doorbells and sleighbells and schnitzel with noodles,
   Wild geese that fly with the moon on their wings,
   These are a few of my favorite things.

My Foolish Heart

Words by Ned Washington
Music by Victor Young

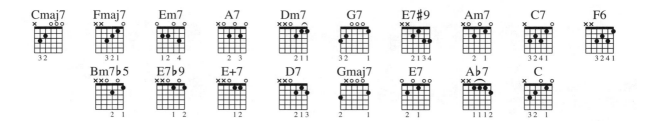

Strum Pattern: 4
Pick Pattern: 3

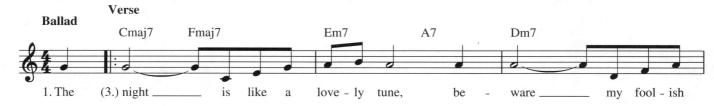

1. The (3.) night _____ is like a love-ly tune, be - ware _____ my fool-ish

heart! How white _____ the ev - er con-stant moon; take care _____ my fool-ish

heart! There's a line _____ be-tween love and fas-ci-na - tion _____ that's hard to

see on an eve-ning such as this, for they both give the ver - y same sen -

sa - tion when you're lost in the mag-ic of a kiss. 2., 4. {His/Her} lips _____ are much too

close to mine, be - ware _____ my fool-ish heart! But, should _____ our ea - ger

lips com-bine then let _____ the fire _____ start. For this time it is-n't fas - ci -

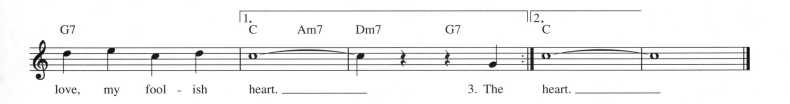

na - tion, or a dream that will fade and fall a - part, it's love _____ this time, it's

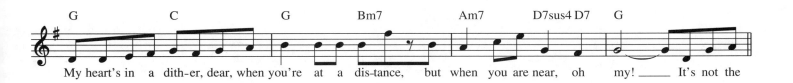

love, my fool - ish heart. _____ 3. The heart. _____

The Nearness of You

from the Paramount Picture ROMANCE IN THE DARK
Words by Ned Washington
Music by Hoagy Carmichael

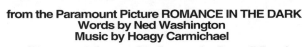

Strum Pattern: 4
Pick Pattern: 3, 4

Verse
Slowly

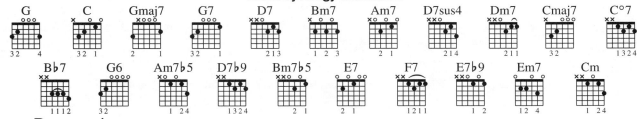

Why do I just with-er and for - get all re-sis-tance when you and your mag-ic pass by?

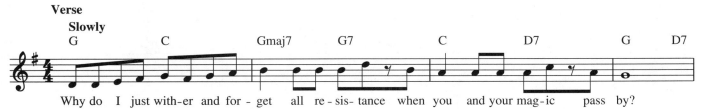

My heart's in a dith-er, dear, when you're at a dis-tance, but when you are near, oh my! _____ It's not the

Chorus

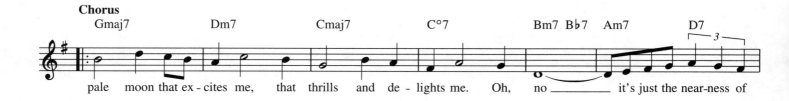

pale moon that ex-cites me, that thrills and de-lights me. Oh, no _____ it's just the near-ness of

you. _____ It is-n't your sweet con-ver-sa-tion that brings his sen -

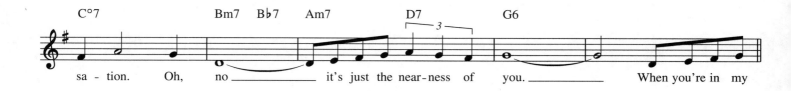

sa-tion. Oh, no _____ it's just the near-ness of you. _____ When you're in my

Bridge

arms _____ and I feel you so close to me, _____ all my wild - est

Outro

dreams come true. _____ I need no soft lights to en-chant me if you'll on - ly

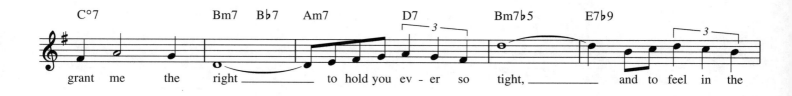

grant me the right _____ to hold you ev - er so tight, _____ and to feel in the

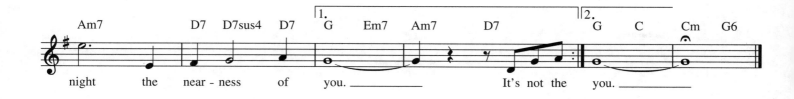

night the near - ness of you. _____ It's not the you. _____

My Funny Valentine

from BABES IN ARMS
Words by Lorenz Hart
Music by Richard Rodgers

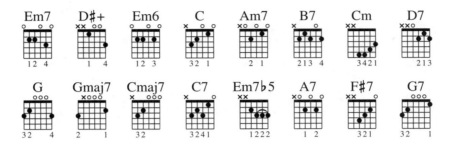

Strum Pattern: 4
Pick Pattern: 5

Moderately

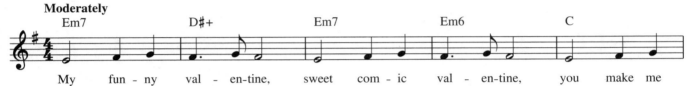

My fun - ny val - en-tine, sweet com - ic val - en-tine, you make me

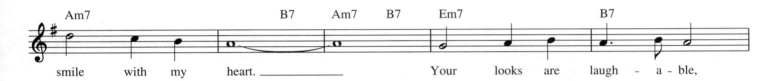

smile with my heart. _____ Your looks are laugh - a - ble,

un - pho - to - graph - a - ble, yet, you're my fav - 'rite work of art. _____

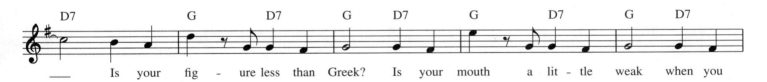

_____ Is your fig - ure less than Greek? Is your mouth a lit - tle weak when you

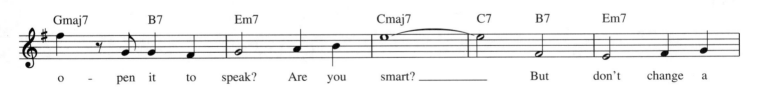

o - pen it to speak? Are you smart? _____ But don't change a

hair for me, not if you care for me, stay lit - tle val - en-tine,

stay! _____ Each day is Val - en-tine's Day. _____

My Heart Stood Still

from A CONNECTICUT YANKEE

Words by Lorenz Hart
Music by Richard Rodgers

Strum Pattern: 3, 4
Pick Pattern: 3, 4

My One and Only Love

Words by Robert Mellin
Music by Guy Wood

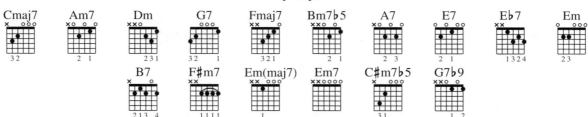

Strum Pattern: 4
Pick Pattern: 5

Verse
Slowly

1. The ver-y thought of you makes my heart sing _____ like an
2., 3. *See Additional Lyrics*

A - pril breeze _____ on the wings of spring. And you ap - pear in all your

splen - dor, _____ my one and on - ly love.

my one and on - ly love. The touch _____ of your hand _____ is like

heav - en, _____ a heav - en that I've _____ nev - er known. The

blush _____ on your cheek when - ev - er I speak tells me that you are my own.

Coda

my one and on - ly love.

Additional Lyrics

2. The shadows fall and spread their mystic charms
   In the hush of the night while you're in my arms.
   I feel your lips so warm and tender,
   My one and only love.

3. You fill my eager heart with such desire.
   Ev'ry kiss you give sets my soul on fire.
   I give myself in sweet surrender,
   My one and only love.

My Old Flame

from the Paramount Picture BELLE OF THE NINETIES
Words and Music by Arthur Johnston and Sam Coslow

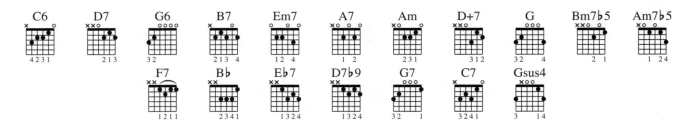

Strum Pattern: 3
Pick Pattern: 3

The mu-sic seemed to be so rem-i-nis-cent; _ I knew I'd heard it some-where be-

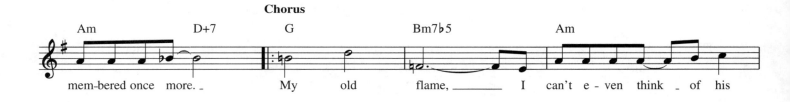

fore. I racked my re-col-lec-tions as I lis-tened, _ when sud-den-ly I ___ re-

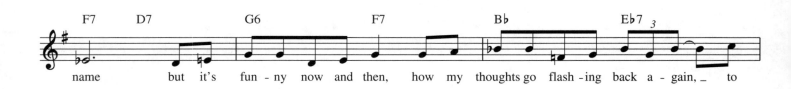

mem-bered once more. _ My old flame, _____ I can't e-ven think _ of his

name but it's fun-ny now and then, how my thoughts go flash-ing back a-gain, _ to

my old flame. _____ My old flame, _____ my

new lov-ers all ___ seem so tame. For I have-n't met a gent so mag-

nif - i - cent or el - e - gant _ as my old flame. _____

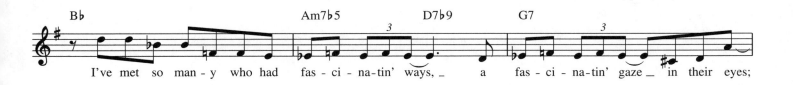

I've met so man - y who had fas - ci - na-tin' ways, _ a fas - ci - na-tin' gaze _ in their eyes;

_____ some who took me up ___ to the skies. _____ But

Outro

their at-tempts at love, were on - ly im - i - ta-tions of my old flame. _____ I

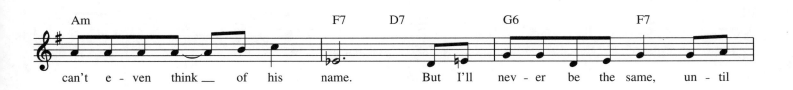

can't e - ven think ___ of his name. But I'll nev - er be the same, un - til

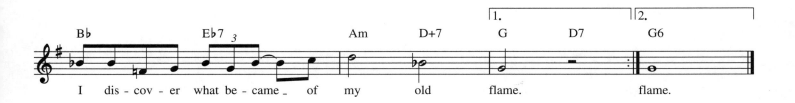

I dis - cov - er what be - came _ of my old flame. flame.

My Romance

from JUMBO
Words by Lorenz Hart
Music by Richard Rodgers

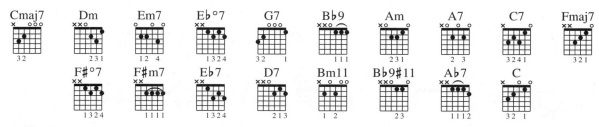

Strum Pattern: 4
Pick Pattern: 4

Verse
Moderately Slow

1. My ro- mance does- n't have to have a moon in the

sky, my ro- mance does- n't need a blue la- goon stand- ing

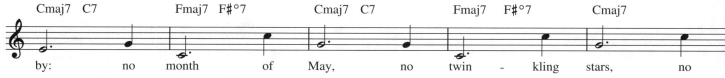

by: no month of May, no twin- kling stars, no

hide a- way, no soft gui- tars. 2. My ro- mance does- n't

need a cas- tle ris- ing in Spain, nor a dance to a

con- stant- ly sur- pris- ing re- frain. Wide a-

wake I can make my most fan- tas- tic dreams come true; my ro-

mance does- n't need a thing but you. _____

My Silent Love

Words by Edward Heyman
Music by Dana Suesse

Strum Pattern: 3, 4
Pick Pattern: 3, 5

Verse
Moderately

1. I _____ reach for you like I'd reach for a star, wor-ship-ping you from a-far,
2., 3. *See additional lyrics*

liv-ing with my si-lent love. love.

Bridge

How I long to tell all the things I have planned. Still, it's

wrong to tell; you would not un-der-stand.

love. _____

Additional Lyrics

2. I'm like a flame dying out in the rain,
   Only the ashes remain,
   Smold'ring like my silent love.

3. You'll go along never dreaming I care,
   Loving somebody somewhere,
   Leaving me my silent love.

Night Train

Words by Oscar Washington and Lewis C. Simpkins
Music by Jimmy Forrest

Strum Pattern: 2, 3
Pick Pattern: 5, 6

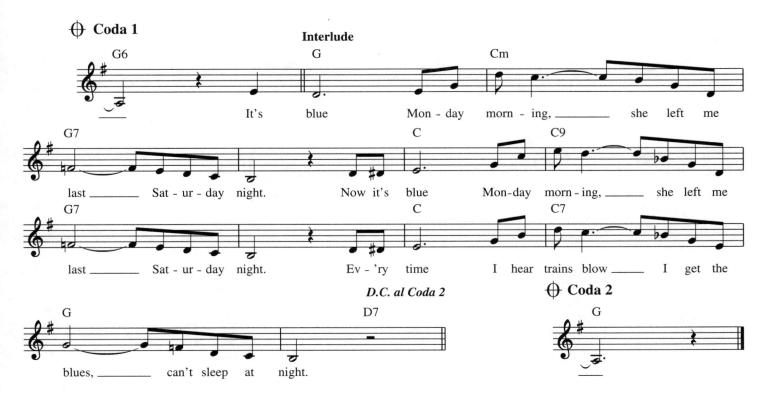

D.C. al Coda 2

It's blue Mon-day morn-ing, _____ she left me last _____ Sat-ur-day night. Now it's blue Mon-day morn-ing, _____ she left me last _____ Sat-ur-day night. Ev-'ry time I hear trains blow _____ I get the blues, _____ can't sleep at night.

Additional Lyrics

2. Night train, your whistle tore my poor heart in two.
   Night train, your whistle tore my poor heart in two.
   She's gone, and I don't know what I'm gonna do!

3. Night train, please bring my baby back home to me.
   Night train, please bring my baby back home to me.
   She's gone, the blues she left just won't set me free.

The Peanut Vendor
(El Manisero)

English Words by Marion Sunshine and L. Wolfe Gilbert
Music and Spanish Words by Moises Simons

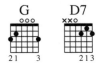

Strum Pattern: 3, 4
Pick Pattern: 1, 3

Verse
Fast Rhumba

1., 3. In Cu - ba, each mer - ry maid wakes up with this se - re - nade:
2. In Cu - ba, his smil - ing face is wel - come most ev - 'ry place;

Pea - nuts! _____ They're nice _____ and hot, pea - nuts! _____ I sell _____ a lot.
Pea - nuts! _____ They hear _____ him cry, pea - nuts! _____ They all _____ re - ply.

bag are call - ing you. Don't waste them no tum - my ache, you'll taste them
pea - nuts good _ to eat. For break - fast or din - ner time, for sup - per, _

when you _ a-wake. For at the ver - y break _ of day, the pea - nut ven -
most an - y time. A mer - ry twin - kle in ___ his eye, he's got a way

- dor's on ___ his way. ___ At dawn - ing that whis - tle blows through ev - 'ry cit - y, town, _
_ that makes _ you buy. ___ Each morn - ing that whis - tle blows. The lit - tle chil - dren like _

___ and coun - try lane, you'll hear him sing his plain - tive lit - tle strain.
___ to trail _ a - long, they love to hear the pea - nut ven - dor's song.

And as he goes by ____ to you _ he'll say: ____ Big Jum - bos, big dou - ble ones,
They all laugh with glee ___ when he _ will say: ____ They're roast - ed, no ti - ny ones,

come buy those pea - nuts roast-ed to - day. _ Come try those fresh - ly roast-ed to - day!
they're toast - ed, pea - nuts hot in the shell. _ Come buy some, I eat more than I sell! _

1st time, D.C.
2nd time, D.C. al Coda

_ If you're look-ing for a mor - al to _ this song, fif - ty mil-lion lit - tle mon-keys can't _ be wrong.
_ If an ap - ple keeps the doc - tor from _ your door, pea - nuts ought to keep him from you ev - er more.

Coda

Pea - nuts! ____ we'll meet _ a-gain. Pea - nuts! ____ this street _ a-gain. Pea - nuts! _

_ you'll eat _ a-gain, your pea - nut man, that pea - nut man's gone.

Out of Nowhere

from the Paramount Picture DUDE RANCH

Words by Edward Heyman
Music by Johnny Green

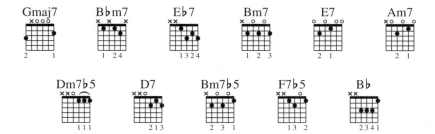

Strum Pattern: 2, 5
Pick Pattern: 1, 4

A Nightingale Sang in Berkeley Square

Lyric by Eric Maschwitz
Music by Manning Sherwin

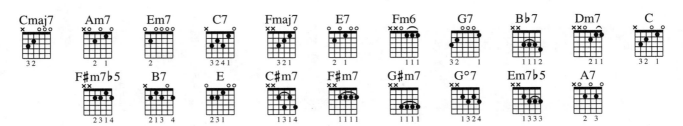

Strum Pattern: 3, 4
Pick Pattern: 1, 3

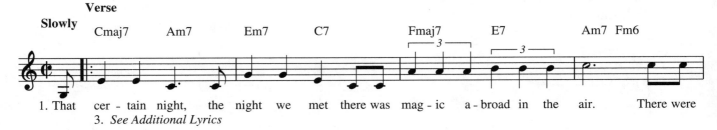

1. That cer-tain night, the night we met there was mag-ic a-broad in the air. There were
3. *See Additional Lyrics*

an-gels din-ing at the Ritz, and a night-in-gale sang in Ber-k'ley Square.

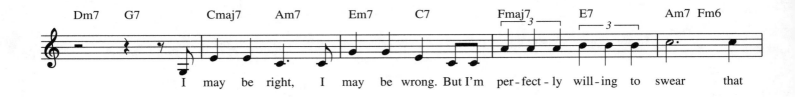

I may be right, I may be wrong. But I'm per-fect-ly will-ing to swear that

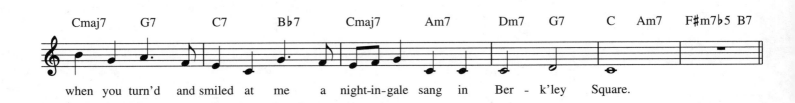

when you turn'd and smiled at me a night-in-gale sang in Ber-k'ley Square.

The moon that lin-gered o-ver Lon-don town, _ poor puz-zled moon, he wore a frown.
See Additional Lyrics

How could he know we two were so in love. _ The whole darn world seemed up - side down. 2.The

Verse

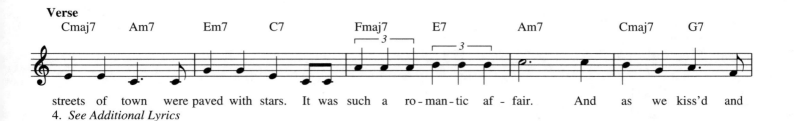

streets of town were paved with stars. It was such a ro - man - tic af - fair. And as we kiss'd and
4. *See Additional Lyrics*

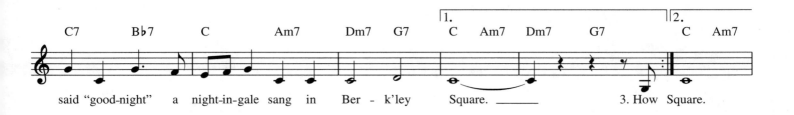

said "good-night" a night-in-gale sang in Ber - k'ley Square. _____ 3. How Square.

I know, 'cause I was there that night in Ber - k'ley Square. _____

Additional Lyrics

3. How strange it was, how sweet and strange.
   There was never a dream to compare
   With that hazy, crazy night we met,
   When a nightingale sang in Berk'ley Square.
   This heart of mine beat loud and fast
   Like a merry-go-round in a fair.
   For we were dancing cheek to cheek
   And a nightingale sang in Berk'ley Square.

Bridge When dawn came stealing up all gold and blue
   To interrupt our rendezvous,
   I still remember how you smiled and said,
   "Was that a dream or was it true?"

4. Our homeward step was just as light,
   As light as the tap-dancing feet of Astaire.
   And like an echo far away
   A nightingale sang in Berk'ley Square.
   I know, 'cause I was there
   That night in Berk'ley Square.

Penthouse Serenade

Words and Music by Will Jason and Val Burton

Strum Pattern: 3, 5
Pick Pattern: 5, 6

Verse
Moderately

1. Pic-ture a pent-house way up in the sky, with hing-es on chim-neys for stars to go by, a
2., 3. *See additional lyrics*

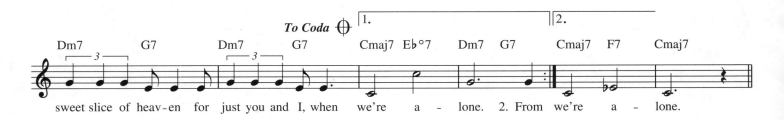

sweet slice of heav-en for just you and I, when we're a - lone. 2. From we're a - lone.

Bridge

We'll see life's mad pat - tern as we view old Man - hat - tan, then we can thank our

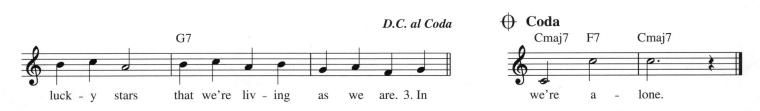

luck - y stars that we're liv - ing as we are. 3. In we're a - lone.

Additional Lyrics

2. From all of society we'll stay aloof,
   And live in propriety there on the roof,
   Two heavenly hermits we will be in truth,
   When we're alone.

3. In our little penthouse, we'll always contrive
   To keep love and romance forever alive,
   In view of the Hudson just over the drive,
   When we're alone.

Poinciana
(Song of the Tree)

Words by Buddy Bernier
Music by Nat Simon

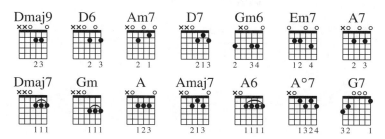

Strum Pattern: 2
Pick Pattern: 2

Verse

Moderately

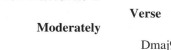

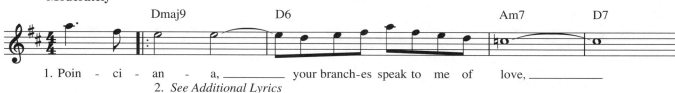

1. Poin – ci – an – a, _____ your branch-es speak to me of love, _____
2. *See Additional Lyrics*

pale moon _____ is cast-ing shad-ows from a – bove. _____ 2. Poin – ci –

beat. _____ Love is ev – 'ry – where, its mag – ic per – fume fills the

air, _____ to and fro you sway, my heart's in time, I've learned to care. _____

Outro

___ Poin – ci – an – a, _____ though skies may turn from blue to gray, _____

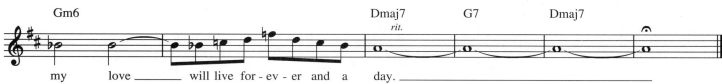

my love _____ will live for – ev – er and a day. _____

Additional Lyrics

2. Poinciana, somehow I feel the jungle heat,
   Within me there grows a rhythmic savage beat.

Satin Doll

from SOPHISTICATED LADIES

Words by Johnny Mercer and Billy Strayhorn
Music by Duke Ellington

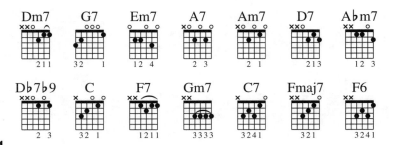

Strum Pattern: 4
Pick Pattern: 1

1. Cig - a - rette hold - er which wigs me, o - ver her shoul - der,
2., 3. See Additional Lyrics

she digs me. Out cat - tin' that sat - in doll.

She's

no - bod - y's fool, so I'm play - ing it cool as can be. _____ I'll

give it a whirl, but I ain't for no girl ___ catch - ing me. _____

Additional Lyrics

2. Baby shall we go out skippin'?
   Careful amigo, you're flippin'.
   Speaks Latin, that satin doll.

3. Telephone numbers well you know,
   Doin' my rhumbas with uno,
   And that 'n' my satin doll.

Softly As in a Morning Sunrise

from THE NEW MOON
Lyrics by Oscar Hammerstein II
Music by Sigmund Romberg

Strum Pattern: 2, 3
Pick Pattern: 3, 4

Verse
Moderately

Love came to me, gay and ten-der. Love came to me, sweet sur-ren-der. Love came to me __ in bright ro-

man-tic splen-dor. Fick-le was she, faith-ful nev-er. Fick-le was she __ and clev-er.

Chorus

So will it be for-ev-er, for-ev-er. __ Soft-ly, as in a morn-ing

sun-rise, the light of love comes steal-ing in-to a new born day, oh!

Flam-ing with all the glow of sun-rise, a burn-ing kiss is seal-ing the vow that all be-

tray. __ For the pas-sions that thrill love and lift you high to heav-en, __ are the pas-sions that

kill love and let you fall to hell! So ends each sto-ry, soft-ly, as in an eve-ing

1.
sun-set, the light that give you glo-ry will take it all a-way. __
2.
way. __

Slightly Out of Tune (Desafinado)

English Lyric by Jon Hendricks and Jessie Cavanaugh
Original Text by Newton Mendonca
Music by Antonio Carlos Jobim

Strum Pattern: 3
Pick Pattern: 3

Verse

Moderate Bossa

Fmaj7 / *G7♭5*

1. Love is like a nev-er-end-ing mel-o-dy; _____
2. *See Additional Lyrics*

Gm / *C7* / *Am7♭5* / *D7♭9*

po-ets have com-pared it to a sym-pho-ny, _____

1.
Gm / *A7♭9* / *D7* / *D7♭9*

a sym-pho-ny con-duc - ted by the light-ing of the moon,

G7♭9 / *G♭maj7*

but our song of love is slight-ly out of tune. _____

2.
Gm / *B♭m7* / *E♭7* / *Fmaj7* / *Bm7♭5* / *E7♭9*

Seems to me you've changed ___ the tune we used to sing; _____

Amaj7 / *B♭°7* / *Bm7* / *E7*

like the bos-sa no - va, love shall swing. _____ We

Bridge
Amaj7 / *B♭°7* / *Bm7* / *E7*

used to har-mo-nize, ___ two souls in per - fect time. _____

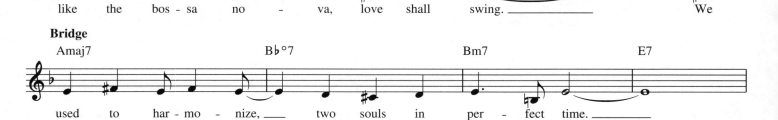

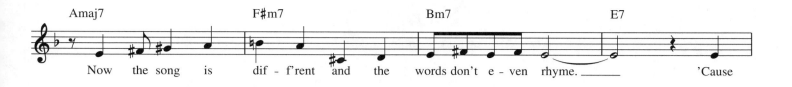
Now the song is dif - f'rent and the words don't e - ven rhyme. _____ 'Cause

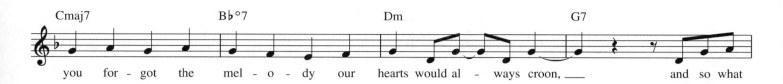
you for - got the mel - o - dy our hearts would al - ways croon, ___ and so what

good's a heart that's slight - ly out of tune. _____

Outro

Tune your heart to mine the way it used to be; _____

join with me in har - mo - ny and sing a song of lov - ing. We're

bound to get in tune a - gain be - fore too long. There'll be

no de - sa - fi - na - do when your heart be - longs to me com - plete - ly. _____ Then you

won't be slight - ly out of tune, ___ you'll sing a - long with me. _____

Additional Lyrics

2. Once your kisses raised me to a fever pitch,
   Now the orchestration doesn't seem so rich.
   Seems to me you've changed the tune we used to sing;
   Like the bossa nova, love shall swing.

Solitude

Words and Music by Duke Ellington, Eddie De Lange and Irving Mills

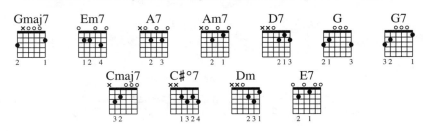

Strum Pattern: 3
Pick Pattern: 3

Additional Lyrics

2. In my solitude
   You taunt me with memories that never die.

3. In my solitude
   I'm praying, dear Lord above, send back my love.

Sophisticated Lady

from SOPHISTICATED LADIES

Words and Music by Duke Ellington, Irving Mills and Mitchell Parish

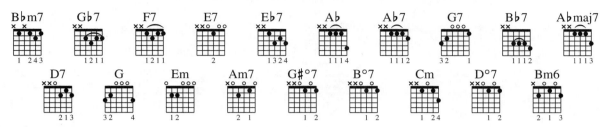

Strum Pattern: 4
Pick Pattern: 4

Verse

Moderately

1. They (2.) say _____ in - to your ear - ly life ro - mance came, _____ and in this

heart of yours burned a flame, _____ a flame that flick - ered one day and died a -

way. Then, _____ with dis - il - lu - sion deep in your eyes, _____ you learned that

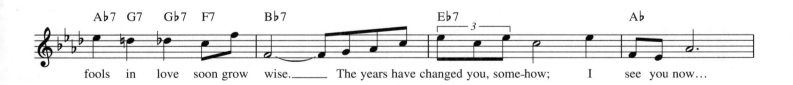

fools in love soon grow wise._____ The years have changed you, some-how; I see you now...

Bridge

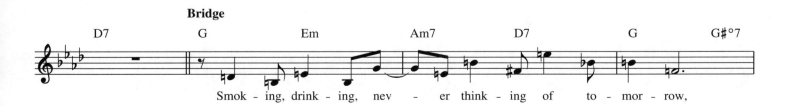

Smok - ing, drink - ing, nev - er think - ing of to - mor - row,

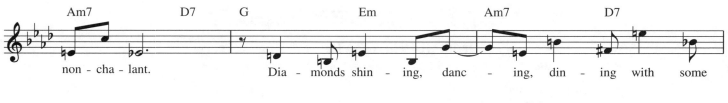

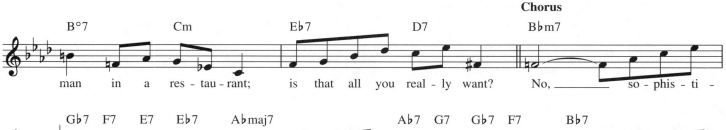

Speak Low

from the Musical Production ONE TOUCH OF VENUS

Words by Ogden Nash
Music by Kurt Weill

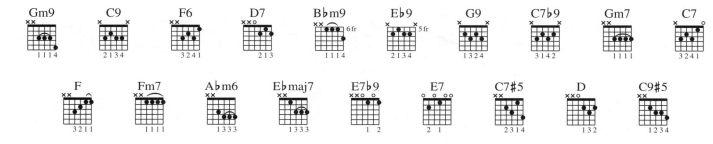

Strum Pattern: 2, 3
Pick Pattern: 4, 5

Verse

Rhumba or Beguine

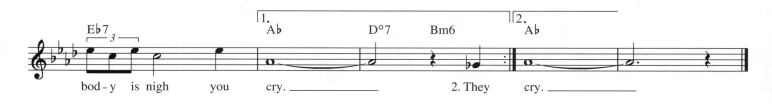

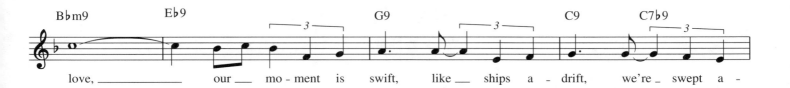

Bb♭m9   E♭9   G9   C9   C7♭9

love, _____ our __ mo - ment is swift, like __ ships a - drift, we're _ swept a -

1.   2.   **Bridge**

F6   D7   Gm7   C7   F   Fm7

drift, too soon. 2. Speak soon. _____ Time is so old _____ and

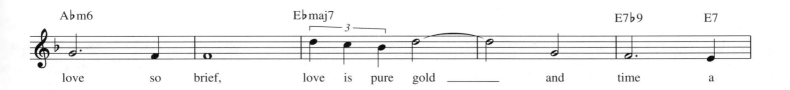

A♭m6   E♭maj7   E7♭9   E7

love so brief, love is pure gold _____ and time a

Outro

C7♯5   Gm9   C9   Gm9   C9

thief. We're late _____ dar - ling we're late _____ the cur - tain de -

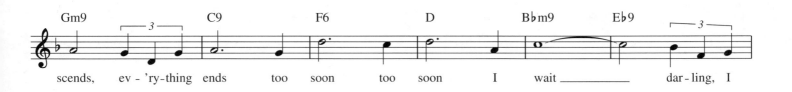

Gm9   C9   F6   D   B♭m9   E♭9

scends, ev - 'ry-thing ends too soon too soon I wait _____ dar - ling, I

F   D7   G9   C9♯5   F6

wait _____ will you speak low to me, speak love to me and soon. _____

Additional Lyrics

2. Speak low darling, speak low
   Love is a spark lost in the dark too soon, too soon,
   I feel wherever I go that tomorrow is near,
   Tomorrow is here and always too soon.

Star Dust

Words by Mitchell Parish
Music by Hoagy Carmichael

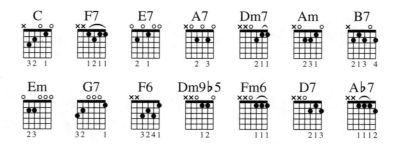

Strum Pattern: 1, 6
Pick Pattern: 2, 5

Verse
Moderately

1. And now the pur - ple dusk of twi - light time steals a - cross the mead-ows of my
2. *See Additional Lyrics*

heart. High up in the sky the lit - tle stars climb,

al - ways re-mind-ing me that we're a - part. the mu - sic of the years gone by. ____ Some-times I

Chorus

won - der why I spend the lone - ly night dream-ing of a song. The

mel - o - dy haunts my rev - er - ie, and I am once a - gain with you, ____ when our

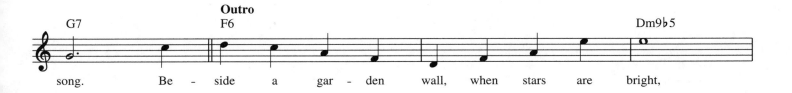

Additional Lyrics

2. You wandered down the lane and far away,
   Leaving me a song that will not die.
   Love is now the star dust of yesterday.
   The music of the years gone by.

Stella by Starlight

from the Paramount Picture THE UNINVITED
Words by Ned Washington
Music by Victor Young

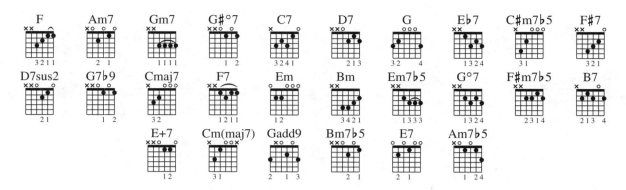

Strum Pattern: 4
Pick Pattern: 3

Moderately Slow

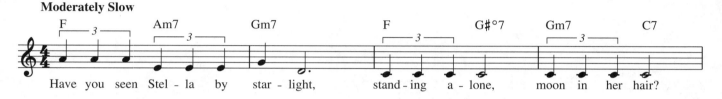

Have you seen Stel-la by star-light, stand-ing a-lone, moon in her hair?

Have you seen Stel-la by star-light, when have you known rap-ture so rare? The

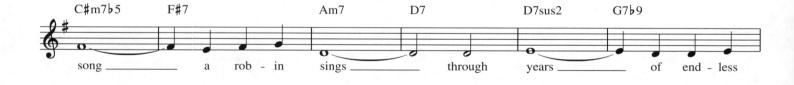

song _____ a rob-in sings _____ through years _____ of end-less

springs. _____ The mur-mur of a brook at e-ven-tide _____

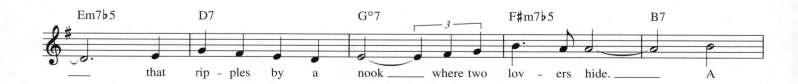

_____ that rip-ples by a nook _____ where two lov-ers hide. _____ A

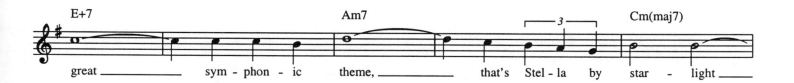

great _____ sym - phon - ic theme, _____ that's Stel - la by star - light _____

_____ and not a dream. _____
Boy: My heart _____ and I a - gree _____
Girl: She's all _____ of these and more. _____

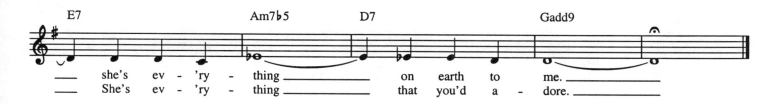

_____ she's ev - 'ry - thing _____ on earth to me. _____
_____ She's ev - 'ry - thing _____ that you'd a - dore. _____

The Very Thought of You

Words and Music by Ray Noble

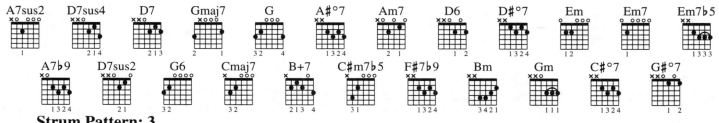

Strum Pattern: 3
Pick Pattern: 4

Verse
Moderately

I don't need your pho-to - graph, _____ to keep by my bed, your pic - ture is

al-ways in ___ my head. _____ I don't need your por-trait, dear, _____ to call you to

mind. _____ For sleep - ing or wak-ing, dear, __ I find: _____ The ver - y

Additional Show Lyrics

I hold you reponsible, I'll take it law.
I never have felt like this before.
I'm sueing for damages, excuses won't do.
I'll only be satisfied with you;

Stompin' at the Savoy

Words and Music by Benny Goodman, Edgar Sampson, Chick Webb and Andy Razaf

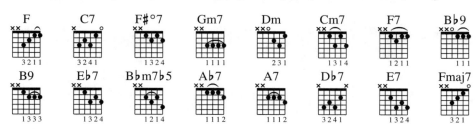

Strum Pattern: 4
Pick Pattern: 5

Additional Lyrics

2. Your form just like a clingin' vine;
   Your lips so warm and sweet as wine;
   Your cheek so soft and close to mine;
   Divine!

Take the "A" Train

Words and Music by Billy Strayhorn

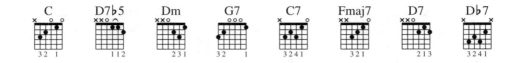

Strum Pattern: 3
Pick Pattern: 3

Verse
Easy Swing

C
1. You _____ must take the "A" train _____
2., 3. *See Additional Lyrics*

To Coda ⊕

Dm   G7   C
to   go to Sug - ar Hill way up in Har - lem. _____

1.   2.

Bridge

Dm   G7   C7   Fmaj7
_____   _____ Hur - ry, _____ get on now it's

D7
com - ing. _____   Lis - ten _____

D.C. al Coda

                     Dm   G7   Db7
to those rails a thrum - ming. _____ 3. All

⊕ *Coda*

C
Har - lem. _____

Additional Lyrics

2. If you miss the "A" train
    You'll find you've missed the quickest way to Harlem.

3. All 'board! Get on the "A" train.
    Soon you'll be on Sugar Hill in Harlem.

Tenderly

from TORCH SONG

Lyric by Jack Lawrence
Music by Walter Gross

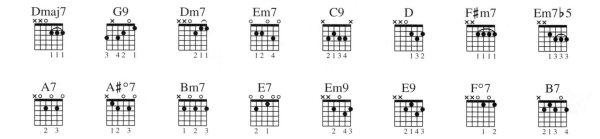

Strum Pattern: 8
Pick Pattern: 7

Tangerine

from the Paramount Picture THE FLEET'S IN
Words by Johnny Mercer
Music by Victor Schertzinger

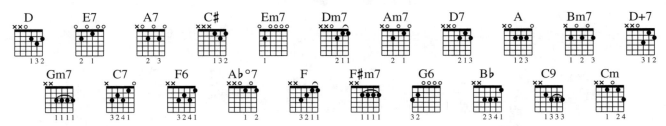

Strum Pattern: 3, 5
Pick Pattern: 1, 4

Verse
Moderately

South A - mer - i - can sto - ries _____ tell of a girl who's

quite a dream, ___ the beau - ty of her race. Though you doubt all the

sto - ries _____ and think the tales are just a bit ex - treme, _____

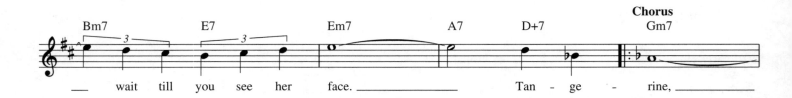

___ wait till you see her face. _____ Tan - ge - rine, _____

___ she is all they claim, _____ with her eyes of night and

Gm7   C7   F   D+7   Gm7

lips   as   bright   as   flame. _____   Tan - ge - rine, _____

C7   F6   E7   A   F#m7

___   when   she   danc - es   by _____   Señ - or - i - tas   stare   and

Bm7   E7   A7   D7   D+7   Gm7

ca - bal - le - ros   sigh. _____   And   I've   seen _____

C7   F6   Ab°7   Gm7   C7

___   toasts   to   Tan - ge - rine _____   raised   in   ev - 'ry   bar   a -

Gm7   C7   A7   D7   D+7   Gm7   _3_

cross   the   Ar - gen - tine. _____   Yes,   she   has   them   all   on   the

Em7   A7   Dm7   _3_   G6   Bb   Gm7

run   but   her   heart   be - longs   to   just   one.   Her   heart   be - longs   to

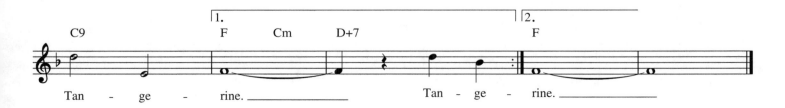

C9   1.   F   Cm   D+7   2.   F

Tan - ge - rine. _____   Tan - ge - rine. _____

There Will Never Be Another You

from the Motion Picture ICELAND
Lyric by Mack Gordon
Music by Harry Warren

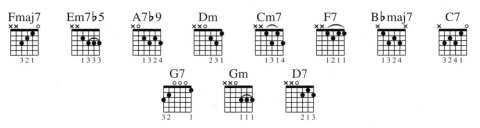

Strum Pattern: 4
Pick Pattern: 5

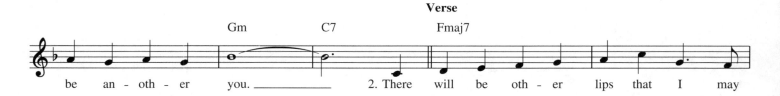

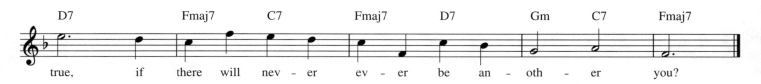

There's a Small Hotel

from ON YOUR TOES
Words by Lorenz Hart
Music by Richard Rodgers

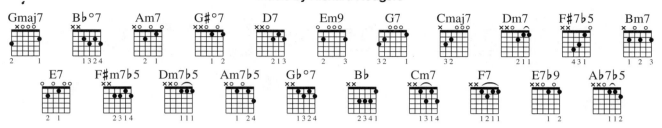

Strum Pattern: 3, 4
Pick Pattern: 1, 3

This Can't Be Love

from THE BOYS FROM SYRACUSE
Words by Lorenz Hart
Music by Richard Rodgers

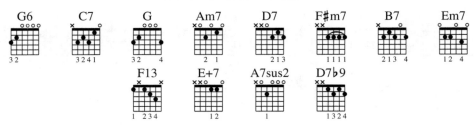

Strum Pattern: 3, 4
Pick Pattern: 1, 6

Moderately

This can't be love be-cause I feel so well, ____ no sobs, no sor-

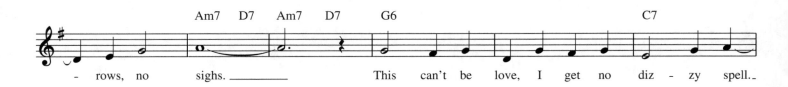

-rows, no sighs. _____ This can't be love, I get no diz-zy spell.

____ My head is not ____ in the skies, _____ my heart does

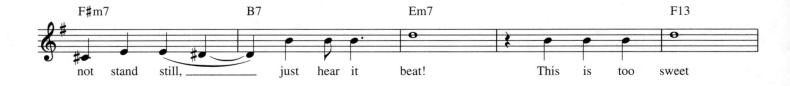

not stand still, _____ just hear it beat! This is too sweet

to be love. This can't be love be-cause I feel so well;

____ but still I love to look ____ in your eyes. ____

Well You Needn't
(It's Over Now)

English Lyric by Mike Ferro
Music by Thelonious Monk

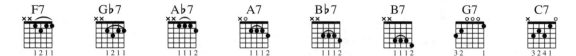

Strum Pattern: 4
Pick Pattern: 3

Verse
Bright Bop

1. You're talk-in' so sweet, well, you need-n't. You say you won't cheat, well, you need-n't. You're
4. *See additional lyrics*

tap-pin' your feet, well, you need-n't. It's o-ver now, it's o-ver now. 2. You're

Verse

dress-in' with class, well, you need-n't. You're hold-in' your sass, well, you need-n't. You
5. *See additional lyrics*

think you're a gas, well, you need-n't. It's o-ver now, it's o-ver now. It's

Bridge

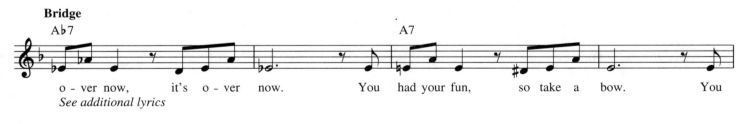

o-ver now, it's o-ver now. You had your fun, so take a bow. You
See additional lyrics

ought-a know you lost the glow, the beat is slow, the shad-ows grow, the lights are low, it's time to go, let's

Verse

close the show down. _ 3. You're tak - in' off weight, well, you need - n't. You're
6. *See additional lyrics*

look - ing just great, well, you need - n't. You're set - tin' the bait, well, you

need - n't. It's o - ver now, it's o - ver now. 4. You're now

Additional Lyrics

4. You're playing a game, well, you needn't.
   It's more of the same, well, you needn't.
   You're coming up lame, well, you needn't.
   It's over now, it's over now.

5. You're bending my ear, well, you needn't.
   You're calling me dear, well, you needn't.
   You're acting sincere, well, you needn't.
   It's over now, it's over now.

Bridge It's over now, it's over now.
   Don't want a scene, don't need a row.
   You had your day, a matinee,
   You had to stray, you know they say,
   You're gonna play, you got to pay, so find a way out!

6. You say that you'll try, well, you needn't.
   You say you won't lie, well, you needn't.
   You're starting to cry, well, you needn't.
   It's over now, it's over now.

What a Diff'rence a Day Made

English Words by Stanley Adams
Music and Spanish Words by Maria Grever

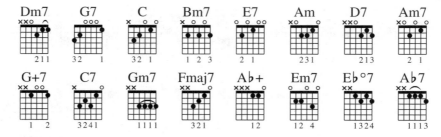

Strum Pattern: 1, 3
Pick Pattern: 2, 4

Verse

Slowly

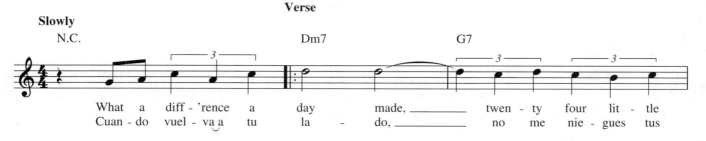

What a diff - 'rence a day made, _____ twen - ty four lit - tle
Cuan - do vuel - va a tu la - do, _____ no me nie - gues tus

When I Fall in Love

from ONE MINUTE TO ZERO

Words by Edward Heyman
Music by Victor Young

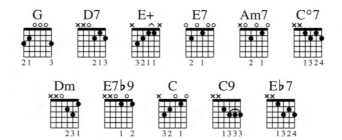

Strum Pattern: 1, 3
Pick Pattern: 2, 3

When I fall in love it will be for-ev-er, or I'll nev-er

fall in love. _____ In a rest-less world like this is, love is

end-ed be-fore it's be-gun, and too man-y moon-light kiss-es seem to

cool in the warmth of the sun. When I give my heart it will be com-

plete-ly, or I'll nev-er give my heart; _____ And the

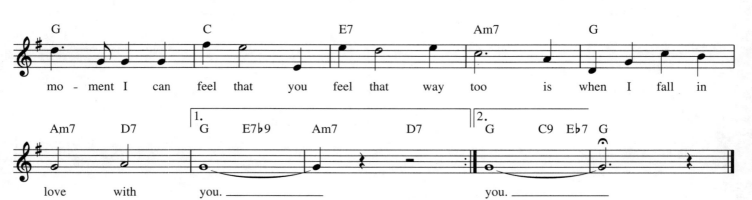

mo-ment I can feel that you feel that way too is when I fall in

love with you. _____ you. _____

When Sunny Gets Blue

Lyric by Jack Segal
Music by Marvin Fisher

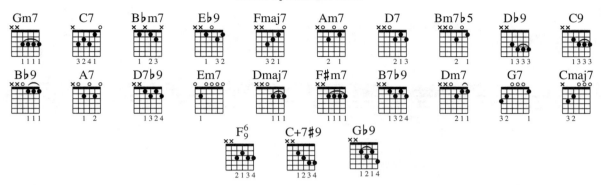

Strum Pattern: 5
Pick Pattern: 3

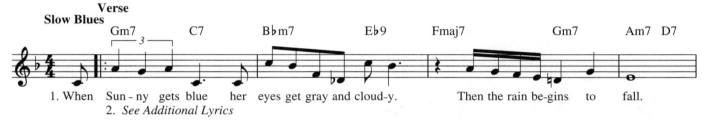

Verse
Slow Blues

1. When Sun-ny gets blue her eyes get gray and cloud-y. Then the rain be-gins to fall.
2. *See Additional Lyrics*

Pit-ter pat-ter, pit-ter pat-ter, love is gone so what can mat-ter? No sweet lov-er man ___ comes to

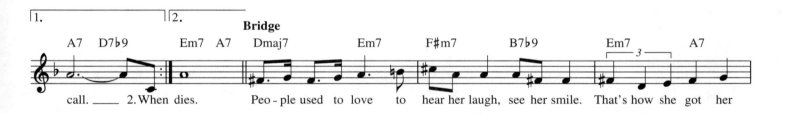

Bridge

call. ___ 2.When dies. Peo-ple used to love to hear her laugh, see her smile. That's how she got her

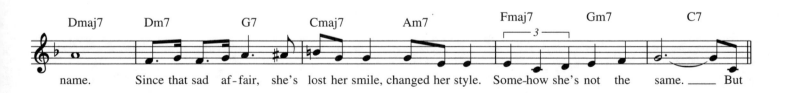

name. Since that sad af-fair, she's lost her smile, changed her style. Some-how she's not the same. ___ But

Outro

mem-'ries will fade, and pret-ty dreams will rise up where her oth-er dream fell through.

Hur - ry new love, hur-ry here_ to kiss a-way each lone-ly tear,_ and hold her near when Sun - ny gets

blue. _____ Hold her near when Sun - ny gets blue. _____

Additional Lyrics

2. When Sunny gets blue, she breathes a sigh of sadness,
   Like the wind that stirs the trees.
   Wind that sets the leaves to swayin', like some violins
   Are playin' weird and haunting melodies.

You Brought a New Kind of Love to Me
from the Paramount Picture THE BIG POND
Words and Music by Sammy Fain, Irving Kahal and Pierre Norman

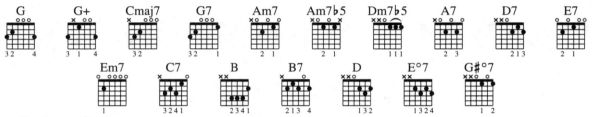

Strum Pattern: 3
Pick Pattern: 1

Verse
Moderately

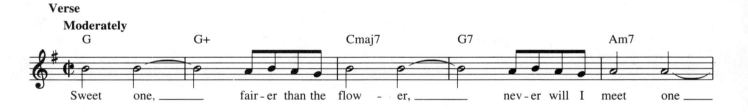

Sweet one, _____ fair-er than the flow - er, _____ nev-er will I meet one _____

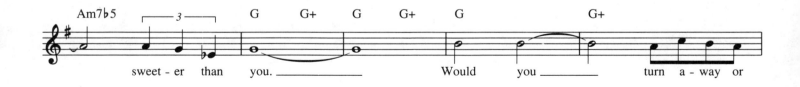

sweet - er than you. _____ Would you _____ turn a - way or

could you _____ real-ly learn to care if I'd ev - er dare to say, "I love you." _____

Chorus

If the night-in - gales __ could sing like you __ they'd sing much sweet - er

than they do. __ For you've brought a new kind of love to me. If the

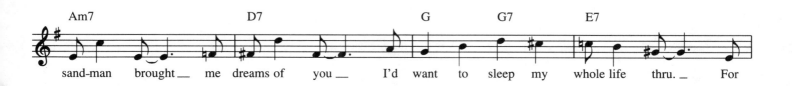

sand-man brought __ me dreams of you __ I'd want to sleep my whole life thru. __ For

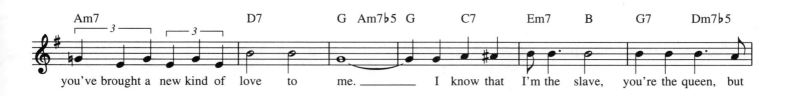

you've brought a new kind of love to me. _____ I know that I'm the slave, you're the queen, but

still you can un - der - stand ____ that un-der-neath it all you're a maid and I am on - ly a

man. I would work and slave __ the whole day thru, __ if I could hur - ry home to you, __ for

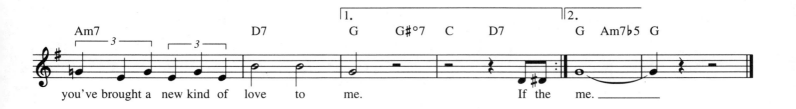

you've brought a new kind of love to me. If the me. ____

Where or When

from BABES IN ARMS

Words by Lorenz Hart
Music by Richard Rodgers

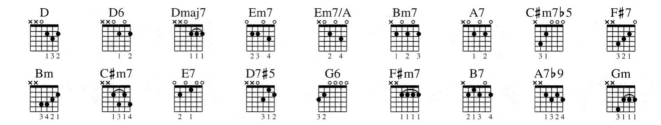

Strum Pattern: 3, 4
Pick Pattern: 4, 6

Verse

Moderately

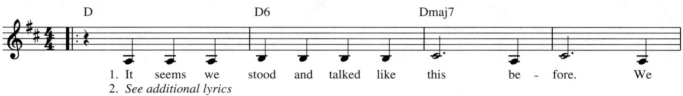

1. It seems we stood and talked like this be-fore. We
2. *See additional lyrics*

looked at each oth-er in the same way then, but I can't re-mem-ber where or

when. _____ when. _____ Some things that hap-pen for the

first time, _____ seem to be hap-pen-ing a - gain. _____

And so it seems that we have met be - fore, and laughed be - fore, and

loved be - fore, but who knows where or when! _____

Additional Lyrics

2. The clothes you're wearing are the clothes you wore.
The smile you are smiling you were smiling then,
But I can't remember where or when.

Whispering

Words and Music by Richard Coburn, John Schonberger and Vincent Rose

P68